Healing Streams in the Desert

Ian M Cartwright

ISBN 978-1-904446-78-1

Printed and published by
Quacks the Printer,
7 Grape Lane,
Petergate,
York Yo1 7hu.
t 0044 (0) 1904 635967 f 0044 (0) 1904 623714
info@quacks.info www.radiusonline.info

Contents

Reactions to Healing Streams in the Desert

This is a story of God's work in the life of a young man from the Black Country, graciously saved and led to full time Christian ministry, although not by the direct route he had expected. Through Deacon Ian's story, both the riches of God's glorious treasure and the fragility of the clay jar in which it is contained are vividly described. Ian's biblical reflection on his ongoing journey into and out of depression, perplexingly and frustratingly recurring throughout his life and ministry, will be a help and a encouragement to anyone who has experienced the bewilderment of Godly ambitions impeded by human limitations.

The pathway to understanding that surpassing power belongs to God and not to us is a painful one, but this account from a fellow traveller makes valuable reading along the way.

Dr. Jeff Clarke

When Ian arrived in York in 2012 he immediately galvanised the church and the community to work together on new exciting and ambitious projects. We had our very own Nehemiah; a man of God with an infectious enthusiasm, drive and passion to grow His Kingdom. Sadly, much like Nehemiah, Ian faced modern day Samballats and sunk down into a very dark place.

I was blessed to meet up regularly with Ian as he battled with depression. These were special times in the coffee shops of York, I was privileged to hear Ian's story and to witness God's healing streams. In every line of this book I can hear Ian's warm dulcet black country tones as he shares his life and learning with clarity, honesty and humour. This is a story of ordinary people and an extraordinary God which can offer encouragement and inspiration for all who journey with Christ. Particularly those who are working to bring growth, change and transformation.

Dr. Russ Smallwood

In this truly insightful book, Ian allows you into his life to discover first-hand the frustrations and joys of struggling with depression. His honesty is everything, as he recounts and reflects upon his journey. No matter how dark the valleys, there is an optimism throughout Ian's writings connected to his Christian faith.
It is with a real sense of thanksgiving that Ian acknowledges the various 'streams' that have been part of his healing process; and it is with gratitude, that we ought to thank Ian for his book – his vulnerably, allows us all to be better informed.
Whether or not you have encountered depression yourself, I would highly recommend Streams in the Desert. Its autobiographical style stops it from being a text book, thus enabling the personal story to speak to the heart. If you are involved in any type of pastoral ministry, Ian's book is a valuable and timely resource.

Simon Rennie, Pastor of York Community Church

This book has rare honesty. It paints life with all its messy complexity yet notices God's love leading. Read and be encouraged.

Reverend Phillip Turner,
Presbyter Minister in the Methodist Church

It was a privilege to read this book about Ian's life; his early boyhood growing up in the Midlands, his first jobs and influences, and the unfolding pattern of how the stresses of life began to affect his health.
Ian deals with his fight against depression with such touching honesty, giving the reader an insight into just how dark and debilitating the illness can be, but then balancing this with the triggers to recovery - through the love of his wife and family, his friends and his deep faith.
Through it all, it is the compassion Ian feels for his fellow human beings that shines through, a gift that will surely ensure fulfilment and better health in the new direction his life and work is taking him now. An encouragement to all who read.

Mrs Jill Solwich, Copmanthorpe Artist

Acknowledgements

A very big thank you to my family and friends for your love and support, and to all those who are dedicated to the pursuit and realisation of new possibilities.

"The joy of the lord is your strength" Nehemiah 8:10.

Foreword

When someone arrives at our centre seeking direction to begin a time of retreat, it is very important to listen to where they are in that moment of their lives. When Ian arrived in 2014, he was in a very difficult space. I suggested, after he settled in, that he look at the story of Elijah in I Kings 19 as a starting point for his reflection and prayer. I had no idea when I offered this to Ian how fruitful and significant this story would become on those days of retreat and in the following months. It was wonderful to see the richness of his prayer at that time as he met a God who wanted to feed, renew and restore him.
Sadly, as for too many people, Ian's desert experience of great hardship was in the church, the pattern of success, opposition, rejection, and renewal that was Elijah's' experience was there for him too, leading to the need to step back, and finally let go of the role of Deacon in the Methodist Church that he trained for and loved. Like many desert dwellers over the centuries, the desert became a place where Ian would encounter the depth of divine love; breakdown leading to breakthrough.
Now the reader has the opportunity to enjoy the humanity of Ian's story, to rejoice in his giftedness, to treasure the honesty and vulnerability, as we hear of his journey with God and the life direction that comes when the dryness of the desert is transformed into a place of healing streams.

Reverend Paul Golightly, Project Director at St Antony's Priory, Durham.

Preface

When I started to write this book I was hurting deeply. The first draft was a dumping ground for all the pain I felt, but it soon became clear that this book itself was a stream of healing. It wouldn't stay put, and became a record of all of God's goodness in my driest places and a signpost pointing to the way ahead.

I've been as honest as I can be in telling my story. I have tried to face up to my own role in how things have developed and I have tried not to blame others. This is my journey, warts and all. This book is not a textbook on stress or depression rather it is a story of what can cause mental and emotional damage to a human being and the healing that is available.

I have heard some Christian preachers encourage people to become Christians by saying, "your problems will disappear and life can become easy, joyous and problem free." From my experience and what I understand about the New Testament, we're told clearly that this isn't quite how things work. Jesus does offer us an abundant life but we may also have to unpack our baggage, discover how to put it down and seize this new life with both hands. Just as we're told Jesus did in John 11:43-44 "Jesus called in a loud voice, 'Lazarus, come out!' The dead man came out, his hands and feet wrapped with strips of linen, and a cloth round his face. Jesus then said to them, 'Take off the grave clothes and let him go.'"

Jesus gave Lazarus new life and then he told the people to take off his grave clothes and let him go. Free from the bondage of the bandages. In the same way, Jesus provides the opportunity for people to receive new life and we work with him to bring release and healing to those we serve.

This is my story. Jesus has given me new life and I've worked with other people to find release and healing for myself, for others and for local communities.

Faith for me is a journey. It doesn't stand still and neither should it. As Christians we are being transformed into the image of Jesus, day by day. And yet we are all human. Most of us fear change and we all react to it in different ways. My journey has been no different in that respect. I have known the sheer joy of walking with Jesus, the love of family and friends. I have seen God bring renewal to churches that were ready to close. I have seen him touch the lives of people who were broken. I have seen him provide for people and communities in miraculous ways.

But I have also seen people knock lumps out of one another in church settings, which has been disappointing to say the least. I had no idea of the devastating effect conflict in the church context would have on me and through it all, I have come to recognise my own personal need for healing.

And so this story is one of healing. My heart has been for the lost in the communities in which I've served. I have seen that some churches need to be renewed in order to reach their communities in new, fruitful ways. However, change brings conflict; they are two sides of the same coin. I am not alone in this, as I know of others who have been faced with fierce opposition and conflict. One of the results of conflict for me personally, has been to slide into periods of deep depression.

The Good News is God gives us everything we need! Throughout my life, God has provided so many opportunities for healing. I view His provision to be like streams of healing in the desert. We all have barren times, times that feel hopeless, times when we want to throw in the towel – desert times. And yet my

experience is that however bad it gets, those streams are never far away, waiting to restore, heal and refresh.
Since starting this book, I have made the decision to retire early on health grounds. I am viewing this as an opportunity to serve in new ways. I don't know where this decision will take me, but I know that I won't be standing still. The journey continues and I believe the best is yet to come.
It is my sincere prayer that my story will encourage others who have been in dark places, places where conflict is rife and where we feel ill equipped to get to our feet, let alone pull others to theirs. I hope that it will encourage people to recognise the challenge ahead and to adapt for it. I pray that it will become a stream of healing to you in your journey with Christ.

God bless you,
Deacon Ian Cartwright.

Introduction

Elijah and Me

'Then a great and powerful wind tore the mountains apart and shattered the rocks before the Lord, but the Lord was not in the wind. After the wind there was an earthquake, but the Lord was not in the earthquake. After the earthquake came a fire, but the Lord was not in the fire. And after the fire came a gentle whisper.' 1 Kings 19 v 11-13

It's one thing to be familiar with a story; it's quite another to live that story. It's true that there's comfort to be found in the familiar. Children love to hear the same tale told over and over. In the living of a story there is something even greater to be found – transformation.

I want to start my story by sharing with you another one. Maybe it's familiar to you. Maybe it will resonate with you. Maybe, to some degree, you're living it – just like I did. It's the story of Elijah and his time in the wilderness.

Elijah was the greatest of God's prophets. He boldly defended the worship of the God of Abraham over the idol Baal, in the North of Israel under the reign of King Ahab.

Elijah had an incredible ministry; so anointed and confident of God's power was he that when he prayed, God caused the rain clouds to dry up and brought fire from heaven. This was a courageous man, who had every reason to depend on the protection of God.

And yet, in 1 Kings 19 we see Elijah driven into the obscurity of the wilderness by the fury of Jezebel, wife of King Ahab, fierce Baal worshipper and persecutor of God's prophets. Here we find a man of staggering faith and confidence, who had prayed so boldly with such miraculous results, now praying to God that he might die! What a terrible place he was in: isolated, depressed, exhausted.

'It is enough!' he said (v4). He felt that he could not do any of it anymore. He was fearful, weakened and tired of conflict. He was burnt out.

We find him under a broom bush where he falls fast asleep. Yet God does not berate him. God does not force him to his feet; instead he sends angels to minister to him.

'Arise and eat because the journey is too great for you.' (v 7) God feeds and waters him in preparation for the forty-day journey to Mount Sinai. He doesn't demand an immediate recovery but ministers to him with great mercy.

We read that God allows Elijah to vent his frustration. As Elijah rages against his suffering, God listens and gives him what He knows he needs – a personal encounter with Him.

Elijah makes his way through the wilderness to Mount Sinai and once there enters a cave. It is during this time in the cave that God appears to him, not in the wind, the fire or the earthquake, not in a dramatic way at all but in that still, small voice. It is that whisper of God, so full of His power and wonder that turns things around.

Elijah leaves the cave and makes the return journey but this time he takes a different route. We read that he meets Elisha and hands to him his prophetic mantle. He has gone from a pioneer to an enabler, encouraging Elisha in his ministry.

It's Elijah's story and yet in many ways it's my story too. What a story! God has used this story to heal many wounds of mine. It has served as a lamp to my feet on many occasions. What a wonderful way for God to speak to me. And it is my prayer that in sharing my story in this book, you might also find encouragement, healing or direction. It is my prayer that you too might bear witness to the power that is the still, small voice of God.

Chapter One
I'll Be a friend

"Be strong and courageous. Do not be afraid or terrified because of them, for the Lord your God goes with you; he will never leave you nor forsake you." Deuteronomy 31:6

Like many stories, mine is about a journey. A journey to high places and low places, green pastures and deserts. It's a journey littered with the questions we all so badly need answering: why does the God of love allow so much suffering? Where is my God of compassion and grace and almightiful love? On a global scale, we ask this when we see natural disasters and when we are surrounded by poor people in desperate need. But on the smaller, everyday scale we're sometimes forced to ask, 'Where's the God of love who loves His Church?' My journey, therefore, has been a search for answers about the nature of God, the nature of my relationship with him but also about the nature of the church and what God is saying to me about it. As a father, He must hate that we, his children, often put one another down and cause damage which can't easily be put right. He loves us so much; how can we help Him heal us? Over the course of my journey I've had answers to some of these questions while others remain, for the moment, concealed.

I started out as a young boy growing up in Tipton; a Black Country lad who paid little attention at school, and who left with no qualifications and seemingly little going for him. I was told often that I was useless and couldn't do anything; that I'd never amount to much at all. But this boy from the Black Country found the Saviour and the Saviour transformed me. In terms of faith, I emerged very slowly, as the shoots of new life do. Yet in the world of work I found my feet rapidly. I remember my very first job. My Dad's hardware store was next to a shop that sold tropical fish; the owner was also a wholesaler to pet shops and had a warehouse nearby. Dad got me a part-time job there whilst I was still at school. I would leave school as soon as I was 15 but I'll tell you more about that later; for now let's just say school and I didn't get on.

I can remember a key moment whilst sweeping the floor in the warehouse when I suddenly thought, finally, this is something I can do. I mean, it's a simple task, sweeping a floor, but it was a real breakthrough for me. It was as if I was transforming the floor with my broom as surely as if I'd been painting it with a brush. It was through that experience and spending time with the people there that I learnt the value of hard work. Suddenly I had a sense of self-worth because I could work, earn money and get on in life. I could amount to something. I wasn't totally useless. Once I realised this, I didn't seem to have an off switch. I became a workaholic. From that moment until recently, I never stopped working. Work was the source and end destination of my personal fulfilment. My be-all and end-all.

Now, I didn't get this work ethic from church – I didn't go to church at that time. I didn't get it from school – my time there was more an endurance test than something formative. Perhaps my parents had an influence here; they always seemed to be just too busy. But largely, the penny dropped of its own accord while I was working at the warehouse; here was a way I could earn a bit of money and start the long process towards independence.

The owner, John was happy about me working there; of course

he was, I was cheap, willing labour. He'd give me as many hours as I wanted. Some weeks I'd do 100 hours; I more or less lived in that place. I was paid 25p an hour at first, which sounds ridiculous now, but to a teenager in the 70s it really was a lot of money. The main thing was, I was happy doing the work and I loved John dearly. He came to fill a gap in my life that I'd been yearning to fill since early childhood.

I really needed this job. Not in the sense that it was the only one I was ever going to get, but more because of the contrast it offered to the misery that was school. There, I was at rock bottom. And as I trudged unhappily through the last two years at school, things seemed to get ever harder. I'd dropped down from the middle of the pack in to a lower ability group and I hated it. I felt as though I shouldn't be there. I felt I was cast adrift. That's why working in the warehouse was my salvation at that time. I still hadn't got any real faith, the church hadn't come into my life then. I do remember on occasions I'd go into the garden and say to myself, 'God where are you, I just need something, I'm desperately lonely.' I was only a kid. I was struggling to make sense of my life and my future. I just remember crying out, but it seemed like I was crying into the void. It just felt really empty. I don't know quite what I was expecting God to do for me, but what I needed was a series of miracles to get me out of that dark place. Did He perform miracles? Over the years He has put opportunities my way time and time again. At first, I didn't see it that way, and barely noticed the changes. But they happened right enough, and in hindsight I would say an emphatic yes, he was answering the pleas I'd choked on in my garden all those years ago.

While God was answering my incoherent and unhappy prayers, I was also slowly but surely inching towards Him. I still hadn't given faith any real thought; I was more concerned with getting my life in order. Slowly, things were working out. I enjoyed working in the warehouse, and I really valued the contribution I was making. I was becoming addicted to work because it masked the pain of failure I was feeling from my wasted school years.

After I'd been working there for about six years I came to realise that the money wasn't that great, and that it wasn't going to get any better. I began to feel used and taken for granted. It might not have been true, but that's how I felt. So there I was, feeling used, putting in all these hours. I thought, 'When will I start being rewarded properly for all this?' I felt as though it was a dead end job. It was the same routine day in, day out. I could see I wasn't going to get anywhere by sticking around. My confidence had also increased; I'd moved beyond the sweeping up, I was warehouse manager now. It was this new found confidence that allowed me to take the next big step on my journey.

At the age of 19, I enrolled in night school for two nights a week. At the time the subject seemed to be a random choice, but with the benefit of hindsight, I can see God's hand at work. I just went along to look for a course and the bloke said, 'Well what about this?' and I said, 'Alright.' And that was that. That was how I stumbled into being an auto electrician. It was a bit of a wrench (no pun intended) because I liked my colleagues at the warehouse. It was a really difficult choice, but I knew I had to leave - I was ambitious and I wanted to better myself. I'd realised, you see, even while I was sweeping the floor that I could better myself. From that moment of realising I could do things, I started to learn. At the warehouse I learnt about running a small business especially as it related to the pet trade. Pet foods, fish tanks and running a warehouse but that was just the start. To become an auto electrician, I had to pass my City and Guilds (vocational qualifications). I worked really hard and started to get a glimpse of the rewards: distinctions and credits in every module. It was surprising and it was wonderful, and it gave me such a boost.

After two years going to college for two nights per week and homework, I finished my City and Guilds and entered my new trade - working in a garage that specialised in car electrics. Compared to modern motors I suppose the wiring looked primitive - there were no computers or engine management systems or other gadgets, but there were still miles of cable in each car, and they had to be connected just so. Mastering these skills gave me a sense of ambition, too. What for, I wasn't quite sure at the time. I knew I wanted to get on, that I didn't want to stop at home. I didn't want to be the Black Country lad who never moved away. I felt as though inside me there were all these untapped resources bursting to be used.

This almost brings me back to the start. I was on a path now, a path that I see that God had laid down for me. But I had totally failed to recognise His hand in it. So He gave me another opportunity to know Him. At around the same time I started working on the cars, I started going to church. I didn't intend to, really, but I wanted to learn to play the organ. The organist at a local Methodist Church was offering lessons, so along I went. I'd go for my lesson and practice at the church. And sometimes he used to invite me to stop and listen to him play, so I would stick around for the odd service. To be brutally honest, as far as I was concerned, the services were dire; I couldn't make any sense of them. It was all jibber-jabber stuff that went straight over my head. I was bored rigid. For some reason, though, I felt a compulsion to carry on. At that time, in that little Methodist Church called Tipton Street there was a group of young people. There was also real identity with other local Methodist churches, especially through the local choir called Rock Foundation. The choir held outings and lots of other events. At Tipton Street we used to go to football matches and bowling together and all sorts. It was just good fun, and in my early twenties, these were the first true friends I'd ever made. I even went out with a girl or two from our youth group (not at the same time though). The thing was I enjoyed all the activities that were associated with the church, but I didn't really get the message at the core of it. I was still going through the motions and yet I just knew there was something more to be had.

That's really how it began for me. This point in my journey was the start of an awareness that there was somebody beyond me who loved me and cared for me. In Deuteronomy, 31:6, it says '...the Lord your God goes with you, he will never leave or forsake you.' So right from the very beginning of my faith, I had a sense that He could be a friend, a real friend, even if I couldn't grasp what was being said in church. I suppose I felt like that schoolboy again, words and lessons just flying past me too quickly so that I couldn't grab hold of anything meaningful. But this time there was hope.

Those few years were a time of really massive change for me; at the start I was broken, although I didn't realise it at the time. I was deeply unhappy, and desperately lonely. Prior to church I'd had no real friends. School was a washout and I had no ambition. I had called out for help at my lowest moments, but couldn't see then what was happening around me. A desire to get on came, once I could see the value of hard work. Things like passing my driving test were real milestones – that was the first exam I'd ever passed! And when I bought my first car, I thought, Wow, I can do this. Most important of all was discovering church, the friends I'd made there and a glimmering sense of the presence of the Lord – this friend who would never leave me. I was trying to get it all straight in my head, and some key people emerged at this time who would help me piece together myself, my life and my faith.

Chapter Two
The Journey Begins

So it was that my experience of church started out with organ lessons. Believe it or not, at that time it was the 'in' thing. I think a lot of people in the mid-70s had organs of one description or another in their homes. My dad was a really good musician - a jazz pianist, and I was hoping some of that would rub off on me. I can't really remember how I found Tipton Street in particular, but I think it was through an advert in the paper. I started to learn. I would go on Sundays to practice and I would sometimes stay to listen to my tutor playing in the services; sometimes I even played in them myself.

I've told you that I found church services really boring, that I couldn't engage with them. I couldn't get my head round what people were up to. I thought I was doing all the right things, making all the right noises. I could go through the rituals but I didn't understand them. To avoid the misery of the Sunday morning service, I changed the time of my organ lessons to the evening, when there were more young people around. As I got more involved, we had lots of fun together enjoying all sorts of fun things. We had a little mission band, that led services at the local Methodist churches and each year we would go on holiday together and we often went to football to watch West Bromwich Albion. But what stands out about this time is that I saw something in their lives that I wanted and needed. Although I was a churchgoer something that they all possessed

seemed to have eluded me.
From my experiences there, I learnt two important lessons that have been part of my missionary philosophy ever since.

1: Church involvement should be fun.
2: That the belonging should precede the believing – that is, feeling safe and secure in a church should be the priority.

These people who had grown up in church families knew something not just because of the rituals but because of their lives. All those mysterious cues - stand up, sit down, speak now, sit here; it was all new to me. I remember on one occasion going to sit down in this pew and someone coming up to me and saying, 'We have our regulars, you can't sit there'. So I moved to a new seat, but I'd sat in someone else's pew. So he moved me again. At the third attempt, I found somewhere that no-one had their name on. This incident didn't really bother me at the time, because I put it down to my own ignorance. But looking back on it, I think it tells me a lot more about what I was going to face in future. About the day-to-day reality of some churches. I felt I was at the door of a great personal change, but I hadn't figured out how to open it. Then I received a great opportunity for growth and learning at the Church. For some reason, I was asked to conduct the annual Sunday School Anniversary service. It doesn't sound like much now, but to the Church at that time and in that place it was definitely a big deal, and something they put a lot of effort into every year. For me, it was terrifying. I didn't have a clue what was going on, but I just rolled my sleeves up and got stuck in. The Sunday School leader introduced me to another Ian. Ian was a little younger than me but a wonderfully gifted musician. We formed this little duo in which he played the piano and I taught the kids to sing the songs. It was great fun. We went on to write our own songs and music for the Anniversaries each year. We worked together for four years, each Anniversary being more ambitious then the one before; they were always a great success.

But I still didn't know what any of it really meant. I used to despair, really. I remember once putting up my hand during the sermon and asking the minister, 'What does that mean?' I was stroppy, in my early twenties and in this little Methodist chapel, just not getting it. The Reverend Paul Smith was the minister there; he was really patient, he had a faithful heart. When I'd ask questions like that, in the middle of the service, he used to say, 'Oh, bless you brother.' He was full of enthusiasm for it, and I think that was the thing that really fascinated me. It was a living faith, and I thought, 'Yeah, that's what I want to be a part of.'

I was desperately looking for something. I think I had a real hunger for God but had no way of experiencing Him. I wanted to right an un-rightable wrong in misspent opportunities at school. That's how I became addicted to work and the pursuit of achievement. I'd been at the garage for a while by that point, and I found identity in grafting. I had hunger, energy, desire, passion and ability.

Then I was made redundant. That was like having the rug taken from under my feet. It felt like a bolt from the blue, and even if you are expecting something like that, it's always a shock. At the time, it really set my confidence back. A few other things were rough in my personal life at that time that I was struggling to deal with. By now I was actively asking myself, 'Where is this God?' I felt He had let me down; my private life was a mess! Sure, I went to church but I still didn't get it. Despite this, I persevered; something deep inside prompted me to. I knew I belonged even if I couldn't properly believe. I forced myself to participate in Church activities. In 1980 Paul Smith arranged a Cliff College Mission for Tipton Street. Cliff is a Methodist lay training centre in Derbyshire. Talk about a living faith! There was something so vibrant and exciting in the students, I just couldn't get over it. Everything in the Bible was real to them and they actually had this tangible relationship with Jesus. They spoke to Him like he was sitting next to them, their best friend. Everything the minister, Paul Smith, had talked about came together in physical form in these people. It was that something I had observed in my new friends in the youth group.

One day during a youth meeting as part of the Cliff mission, this guy gave his testimony. He told us about how he felt he had been let down by God. He told us about how his relationships had gone wrong at home. Then he told us how he had just cried out to God one night, 'Where are you God? I need you in my life. This seems so wrong, why shouldn't I just walk away from it?'

I was amazed. His story completely resonated with mine. It was weird, as if the whole evening was designed to bring me to a full realisation of the power of God. It was like I was the only person in the room. I too had prayed prayers like this, prayers formed from hopelessness and brokenness, from desperation. Maybe mine could also be answered.

Later that week I went to the final service of the mission. During a hymn Paul Smith made an appeal for people to come and kneel at the communion rail if they wanted to ask Jesus into their life. Paul had always talked about salvation, talked a lot about the Cross and the death that Jesus had died for me. I'd known it in my head but not in my heart. During the previous few days I had thought about little else except that man's testimony. I'd shed my inhibitions and knew it was finally time to let go and answer the call.

I found myself staggering up to the communion rail, stunned by everything that was going on. Once I got there, I made my confession, and let Jesus into my life. It was as if a weight had been lifted off me. I knelt there and I wept and wept. I cried my eyes out. I just felt overwhelmed by emotion and love. Paul laid his hands on my head and he said, 'Just accept Jesus into your life, He died for you, just accept him in, it's easy; it's as easy as ABC - Accept Him into your life, Believe in Him for all you need and Confess it to another – Tell someone you have been born again because you have asked Jesus to come into your life.' My first love of the Lord was based on the Cross, Jesus's death and resurrection. It was all free and it was sufficient for me. Jesus' sacrifice and purchase of salvation for me produced new life, new opportunities and fresh starts.

I had been standing in the porch before, waiting for someone to let me in. Now I realised the door had been open all the time, and it had been me who had been refusing to take that last step. I had been a churchgoer, but I hadn't really become a Christian. Now I stepped over the threshold and responded to the opportunity God had been trying to grant me for years. Paul would say, 'What's heavy on your heart right now?' For me there was so much. What could I do? What could Jesus do? I was born again.

Afterwards, I found this thing became all-encompassing. Not the church stuff, but Jesus. I had a little Mini 850cc, and the Slade cassettes all got put to one side, as I started listening to Christian musicians. There was a song I used to listen to a lot at that time, by a guy called Dave Pope, called 'I'll Be A Friend'. The lyrics really spoke to me. I played this song all the time in my car and at home. It went like this:

People come running whenever there's money
And friendship is not hard to find
When it's all gone away, hardly a soul will stay
Friendship can be so unkind
They say a friend in need is a friend indeed

And I need someone I can trust with my life
And I've found him

I'll be a friend to Jesus, long as I live
I'll be a friend, give him all I can give
I'll be a friend oh, what a friend he's been to me
I'll be a friend to Jesus all of the time
Give him my life, my body, soul and my mind
I'll be a friend oh, what a friend he's been to me

Some may be friendly just to be trendy
While others may just past the time
Some will be friends to achieve their own ends
While others can't make up their own minds
They say a friend in need is a friend indeed
And I need someone I can trust with my life
And I've found him

I'll be a friend to Jesus, long as I live
I'll be a friend, give him all I can give
I'll be a friend oh, what a friend he's been to me
I'll be a friend to Jesus all of the time
Give him my life, my body, soul and my mind
I'll be a friend oh, what a friend he's been to me

I also started to write my own songs a bit more, and they had more impact. Ian used to write the music and I would put some words to it.
After being reborn, I had an unquenchable thirst for the Lord. I immediately wanted to go to Cliff College and learn more about my newly discovered faith. The people at Cliff said I had

to wait for a year to see if this really was my calling, which was hugely frustrating. In the meantime I was becoming more and more entrepreneurial and had a host of ideas to fill that time and provide for myself. With my redundancy money I bought a minivan and did work outside people's houses, on their cars. If you were around in the 1980s, you might remember Norman Tebbit, Tory MP for Chingford in Essex. He was pretty uncompromising, and as well as being described as a 'semi-house-trained polecat' had invited the unemployed to do like his father, who had, '...Got on his bike to look for work, and he kept looking until he found it.' That's what I did. Now, I'm not much of a Tory, definitely more red than blue but I was thinking, 'OK, I'm in this position, what am I going to do about it?' And while I was running my own auto electrical business, I continued the fellowship and experienced the joy with those young people at the Sunday evening Bible studies and sharing. That was really important, the fellowship and fun with them.

The year passed pretty quickly and I was finally allowed to attend Cliff College. Those students I'd met during the Cliff College mission at Tipton Street had had a compelling faith. Cliff is a fantastic place in the Peak District, with its own grounds, which at that time welcomed a wide range of students from various parts of the country and from overseas. When I went to Cliff, I had the time to discover a bit more about the Bible; I had such a hunger and thirst for the refreshing presence of His Holy Spirit. My year at College was a GAP year, where study was the release from my normal life. It was a really hopeful time for me in stark contrast to my school days. At college I had done well and obtained good results from my City and Guilds and after that I had learnt a lot about running a business. So at Cliff I once again threw myself into learning. People that I knew as friends at Cliff are still friends now, all these years on.

The whole thing was like that first love for me.
During my year at Cliff we had a guest speaker for a weekend. A great man, Reverend Selwyn Hughes, who was to have a big influence on my life. He was a Welsh firebrand preacher, and a Pentecostal minister. His theme for the weekend was healing and he would talk about healing in terms of Biblical Therapeutics. I wondered, 'What on earth? What could that mean?' I came to realise it was all about the healing power of God. How the Bible is the written word of God and can bring real healing. Healing of the body and of the mind. For me, that was really important because for the first time I had found a means of dealing with some of the things in my past; of finding and giving forgiveness.
This idea of inner healing had planted a seed, which wouldn't flower for some years. Although I had a lot to work through from my past and my present, I probably wasn't ready to face all of it, and I now see that real healing takes a lot of time and effort. Once again, God was answering my prayers; not in the way or the timeframe I wanted, but in the way that worked out best for me.
Most importantly at Cliff, I met my wife Alison. She was working as the Principal's Personal Secretary and it became quickly apparent that we clicked. Alison has been a rock in the ups and downs of my life, and I couldn't have done anything in this book without her love and support.
I'd had a remarkable couple of years – being born again, meeting the wonderful Paul Smith and Selwyn Hughes, wonderful friends at Tipton Street and the Sedgley and Gornal Circuit of the Methodist Church and meeting and falling in love with my wife. I was deepening and broadening my love of God, encountering Him through study, prayer, worship and fellowship. I had had a tough time being made redundant but I had emerged a stronger character for it.

And things were about to move on. On leaving Cliff, I was ready. Ready to take my faith to the next level.

Chapter Three
Decisions and Consequences

"You are not where you once were. You are not where you're going to be. You are in a confusing zone. Welcome to the Land Between." Jeff Mannion.

The next phase of my story lasts 15 years, and although I'm going to whizz through it, it's not unimportant. It was an essential period of growth, transformation and healing that I'd previously avoided. I needed this in three areas of my life: my life as a Christian, my life as a husband and father, and my life as a breadwinner. If you were there, it might have been difficult to see the transformation day-by-day. It's only when you look back that you see how far you've come.

I really felt, as I entered Cliff College that I was at the start of an amazing and transformed life, a life of service, dedicated to the Lord. I had no idea how right I was! What I also didn't realise was just how long it would take to get there. There was work to do. With the help of Jesus, my wife Alison, friends and family, I emerged a better person at the end of it. But like the Israelites, who wandered in the land between two places for forty crushing years after leaving Egypt, I didn't realise how much healing was needed. How much of the past I needed to put behind me. How much I needed to forgive. And how slow the mills of God can grind.

So there I was, finally starting on my new life. Cliff College in

Derbyshire was going to take me as a student for a year. I was thrilled. It was so exciting – living away from home for the first time, meeting new people and learning more about the Bible and its teachings. I was a new Christian, just 2 years in; the idea of going to Cliff was to learn more about my relationship with God, to deepen my faith and to explore what options were open to me after that year. Cliff is different now to how it was then. Nowadays you can do degrees and all sorts; you couldn't then. It was a basic one year course, and you attended lectures in Old Testament, New Testament, worship and preaching, Christian doctrine and church history. It was all pitched at entrance level, which was ideal for where I was. I saw it as a chance to learn about my faith and how to share it with others. You did get a certificate at the end but I'm not sure it meant all that much academically. To me, however, it meant everything. I was also awarded a college prize for improvement in English language.

We weren't just sitting in the lecture hall, though; there was a practical side to the learning experience. We went on mission to different places. I did a weekend at a place called Cleckheaton in Yorkshire, I went to Nantwich on a ten day Easter Mission and then in the summer I was part of a team that served for two weeks in Sheffield and then a week at Ripon in Yorkshire.

During the year I was able to take on preaching appointments in little country chapels in the area surrounding Cliff. There was also manual work to be done. Mine was in the Audio-Visual team, and it turned out to be one of the best assignments of my life.

I worked in a small team, recording services and events onto tape, then duplicating them for customers. It was an easy role and I felt privileged to be able to do this work as other students did gardening, washing up and all sorts of other hard manual work. I was blessed.

One of my jobs was to post the catalogue of cassette tapes that the college held in stock. In the early eighties, we didn't have a photocopier but a mimeograph machine called the Gestetner. It had this great big drum you'd have to work by hand. It was a pain, really but fortunately for me, this Gestetner was located in the Principal's secretary's office, where a young lady called Alison worked. I thought she was lovely. I began collecting as many of the cassette catalogues as I could so that I could see her and chat to her while we were running off these copies. I used to insist on going to get these catalogues, which Alison had produced, myself. In the end I amassed piles and piles of paper that nobody would ever need. The day we left we opened a cupboard and it was full of catalogues!

After a while we started seeing a bit of each other. I was a student living in the college's accommodation. She was Dr Wood's secretary, and lived in a cottage in the grounds. Back then it was quite an old-fashioned sort of place so the idea was you had to be in the building by 10pm. This was a bit early for me, so Alison gave me a door key to the Joyful News Door, as it was named, so I could get back in. Not very late I hasten to add, but late enough when everybody else had to be in bed.

Eventually that 'GAP' year at Cliff had to finish, but it was still an exciting time. I was falling in love and also wanted to explore ministry a bit further. Alison and I got married at Cliff College a year after I left, in 1984. I had spent a year in a lay worker's role in the church, but by then I was working for a power-tool hire company in the workshop, repairing tools. It was something I could do easily, so I soon picked it up. We both had cars so we sold one of them to put a deposit on a house in Ilkeston. We moved into our own home after our honeymoon in Guernsey. It's not a very salubrious place, Ilkeston, but that's where we started out and it suited us fine.

There's always that getting-to-know-you stage, when you first get married and you acclimatise to each other's ways. That's always an interesting journey, that first year or so. In fact, I don't think it ever ends - you continue to discover things about one another. Even now things come along with an 'Oh!' Our 33 year-long relationship has been a very positive experience, with ups and downs that have allowed us to learn and grow together.

After three years of married life, we moved to Derby. Our son, David, had been born in 1985, and we lived in Derby for the next fifteen years. When David was born, I wanted to be the best dad I could be. I wanted to be there as much as I could and do the right things the right way. I had been blessed by a number of role models, observing people whom I respected but nobody's ever written the perfect parenting manual. I think if you can put your head on the pillow at night and think, 'That was good enough,' then you've probably done all right. I can honestly say with David, we had no trouble with him at all. We've been very blessed.

When David was born, Alison and I made the decision that she should stop working so she could be at home with our son. Financially it was a real struggle, as I wasn't on great money in the power-tool workshop. We wanted to give David a sense of security and identity and we wanted to do our best for him.

Our family life has evolved over the years, but Alison and I have always been very best friends and that is a good basis for any marriage. It's been a stabilising influence for us. David's part of that friendship; I'm his dad but he's my friend as well. I love Alison to bits still and we've had a really good life together. What's more we're still going strong!

But back to those early years, when Alison and I were still getting to know one another. It was then that I had my first big setback since leaving home. I'd completed my year at Cliff and felt I was ready to take a role within the church. After college, most people went back home to their day jobs, some went abroad, some did further training at other colleges. I applied for several positions and secured a lay worker's role in the Ilkeston Circuit of the Methodist Church. Qualification-wise, all I had was a piece of paper from Cliff which then had no academic value and my City and Guilds in vehicle electrics. The Cliff College certificate meant everything, because it was the first thing of note I'd done in my journey towards ministry. I've still got that certificate on my study wall; it reminds me how far God has brought me.

Lay employee roles within the Methodist Church have got much better as the years have moved on. Back in the eighties they were still new so I think my generation paved the way and made it better for those that followed. It really wasn't ideal in terms of the employment conditions. In hindsight, I can see now that I knew I wasn't ready for ministry. Thirty years later, I'm an ordained Methodist Diaconal Minister with a lot more experience. I realise that at that time, I wasn't ready, either as a person or as a Christian. What I really felt in my heart was that I'd found this wonderful thing called Christianity, and I knew I wanted to be in full-time paid Christian work. This lay role was not something I had to take up; I chose to. I think it was a decision that I made because I didn't want to go back home to the West Midlands. By going to Cliff, I'd moved away from home; I needed to continue and forge my own life. After that experimental year of being a lay worker, though, there wasn't any other option but to go back into industry. I just hadn't got the personal resources needed for ministry; I was a young Christian but I was still quite bruised from my childhood.

For a while, I was deeply disappointed that I couldn't follow the planned trajectory and go into the ministry. I felt as though that avenue had come to an end before it had really got going. I was disappointed, frustrated, and angry too; I think this fresh anger was hooking into stale, unresolved anger from my past. I remember talking to peers and ministers and they were saying that I needed more experience. Also, because of what I'd learnt at Cliff, I was aware that there was some healing to be done. Some inner healing needed to take place and the lay worker job in Ilkeston had only reinforced that. I needed to find some counselling, some support and some peace in myself, really. Looking back at how I reacted, I was immature, very insecure and had no real self-awareness.

Now that I'd been knocked back, it was time to rebuild. Family life massively changes all of us, yet it gave me a real sense of identity and security. The love I'd felt from the people at Tipton Street all those years before was magnified and became really personal with Alison. I was welcomed into her family as well. They are all very special.

So I'd more or less finished off my year's contract in Ilkeston, but I was looking for other things. I'd started working for the tool hire firm before I'd finished the lay worker's job, because that wasn't a sustainable income or career path. So for the time being, I was quite content to find this job fixing power tools for a family business. It seemed like an opportunity to do something else and potentially map out a life for me and my family.

But I still had a problem. I was increasingly aware that I wasn't ready to fulfil my calling to ministry, but I always felt a pull to it in my heart. I could quell it briefly with a course or a retreat. But in the end it always came back. During this time at the tool hire company, I managed to rise through the ranks – from the workshop, to the front desk, sales rep, depot manager and finally general manager of the Events and Site Services department. There too, each sales target or promotion would briefly damp down the voice urging me to follow my true path, find peace in my heart and the fulfilment I yearned for. Someone once said to me that I would `never know peace until

I was engaged in fulltime paid Christian ministry'. I needed to plan, to accumulate experience. So I did some further study and some training. A significant piece of training was through an organisation called Wholeness Through Christ. The organisation had been recommended to me for its approach, which combined teaching, experience and personal therapy. The courses were weekly residential sessions at retreat houses. I found the courses really liberating and freeing. What still sticks in my mind was the framework they used. They looked at 4 areas:

1: An activating event and the emotion that came out of it (wounds)
2: Bondage, when one becomes gripped by what has happened (captivity)
3: Forgiveness
4: The enemy and how he can put his claws into our wounds, our captivity and our lack of forgiveness.

This model became really important to me. I was hurting and felt bound by some of the things from my past. Ultimately I needed to forgive and be freed from the power of the evil one. That course was an introduction into something that was really personal and very powerful. I am very thankful for the ministry of Wholeness Through Christ.

I spent some time at St John's College in Nottingham, on an introduction to Pastoral Counselling and a course called 'Journey Through Life'. The two courses together formed a diploma in pastoral care and counselling. Those were my first formal qualifications in Christian ministry. I also went on an 'Introduction to the Bible' course, and sessions on particular books from the Bible that I wanted to study. In addition to this I completed a module on Paul's letters at London Bible College (now the London School of Theology).

So I was doing lots of different things, and I was also involved as a layperson in the local Methodist church in Derby. I helped run some local courses on pastoral care for the circuit. I helped write the course with a small team and Alison put the course notes together.

The small team delivered the courses on Saturdays. We recorded the sessions on video and audiotapes so people could have access to the material in house groups or for personal use. We also had children's ministry so people could attend as families. I hoped it helped the people we engaged with. I know that it really helped my development. As a lay person, I was gaining experience and training in my own time at my own cost, and got a profound sense of fulfilment from that.

As time went by I became a Methodist local preacher. I didn't do a lot of preaching then, three or four appointments a quarter maybe, but it was enough. I was gathering experience, and was involved in the local church.

When you put all that together there was a lot of work: a full time job, family and wider involvement in the life of the church. As I've said, I had a tendency towards workaholism and if anything, it was getting worse. I was still trying to straighten what was crooked, I realise that now. I wanted to make something of my life; I was ambitious in everything I did, everything was a competition. Everything was about success.

Alison supported me through all of this. She's always been supportive. For her it's always family, first and foremost. As a family, whatever we did we had to do together. While I was climbing the ladder at the tool hire firm, I would also look for jobs with Christian organisations such as Scripture Union and Crusade for World Revival (CWR). I went for a couple of interviews at CWR but none of those doors opened. There was a sense of frustration there though the promotions at work offset that for a period. To be honest, I think it was God making me wait, like the Israelites had to wait before entering the Promised Land. He knew how much work was needed before I would be ready, and preparation takes time. Basically I had to keep working to hide the pain and stay in that land between two places, trusting in God to provide.

Every time I did well at work, it gave me great satisfaction, but I couldn't keep a sense of unease away for long. The sense of calling was strong within me, and I couldn't find true fulfilment in work no matter how many hours I put in or how many sales targets I smashed. Ultimately, this was to be the cause of my first breakdown.

Chapter Four

My First Breakdown

Teach us, good Lord,
To serve you as you deserve;
To give and not to count the cost;
To fight and not to heed the wounds;
To toil and not to seek for rest;
To labour and not to ask for any reward,
Save that of knowing that we do your will.
St Ignatius Loyola (1491-1556)

I had to make a long emotional and spiritual journey after leaving Cliff College. I thought I was growing and developing all that time and to an extent I was. But the loneliness of the lay worker's role had been a shock to me after the joy of Cliff College. To overcome this disappointment, I knuckled down to set my family up, to do the right thing and to explore my faith and calling. It's odd, but, the thing I thought I had the most control over, my work in tool hire, turned out to be my biggest weakness. In the end I had a total meltdown; mainly because I still lacked the self-awareness to understand what was truly driving me.

I've explained how I used to work long, hard hours as a structure to support my search for identity and recognition. It was a domain I could control, and I realised that if I worked harder and for longer than anyone else, the tangible reward would be a bonus or a promotion. But this ethos stopped me from seeing myself. I didn't know who I was, that was the thing. I allowed my drive and ambition to misdirect my attention.

Still, the tool hire place took me on, promoted and trained me. For them I was an ideal employee, and the reward I got from working with them muted the nagging call to full time paid Christian service. For a while, anyway.

In those early days, I didn't have any real expectations about where I would end up. I didn't know how long I would be at it as I still felt drawn to the church, really. I started off in the workshop fixing customer repairs and maintaining the hire fleet kit. Later on I started helping out generally as I learnt more about the job and the industry. I went on to the front counter, the hire desk. I served customers and answered the phone. I took deliveries for the drivers. I was acting as assistant manager if you like. The promotions went on and because I was good in the shop and good with the customers, I went on the road as a salesman. That was a real step up. My first white collar job; now I had to go to work in a suit and tie. I was chuffed to bits when I got my first company car, a Ford Sierra. I remember it had a car phone in it, which was really flash in those days. The car had leather upholstery and all the bells and whistles that went with it, it was really lovely. I was out selling our products and services in Derby and Loughborough, but because I'd had experience of working in the shop and workshop, I filled in a little bit in those two depots as well. Then I was a salesman at head office in Nottingham, Long Eaton, and the shop in Bulwell. As the company grew they opened new depots and shops in various towns around the East Midlands. I'd go and help start those new depots, or when they took over a depot from another firm, I'd help the transition into our business. Then I'd go out to meet the new customers and do some work around and about

the area.
I was good with people, so managing and selling suited me well. A director, who was a good salesman mentored me and took me under his wing quite a bit. He was likeable - a people person, and I learnt a lot from him about selling and managing the business. The good thing about that company was that they always tried, wherever possible, to promote from within. They had brought in managers in the past and it hadn't really worked. The outsiders just didn't get the company. There were some of us who all started at the roughly the same time, and we all got promoted together as well. We all grew with the company.
Eventually I was made depot manager in Bulwell. That was the first shop I ran by myself. Me and the other lads there grew the business so we were able to move from the small shop to a larger shop. It seemed too good to be true in a way, and I've since heard it said that if something looks too good to be true, it most probably is. The firm had grown larger and larger during the long boom years of the nineties. The company was adding stores and new divisions to the business, but in the end, they couldn't take it any further by themselves. So they looked elsewhere for new investment, and decided to float the company on the stock market. The company changed overnight, and I started to feel again this sense of dis-ease, not only about personal fulfilment but, for the first time, with the company.
It was around this time that I began to be bullied. This was the first time I'd been bullied since leaving school. The person in question had been with the company for some time and despite my previous sales record, suddenly I couldn't do right for doing wrong. He made my targets so high it was unrealistic, and just kept on at me if I couldn't meet these ridiculous standards. I was thrown right back to those unhappy school days and this unsettled me deeply. I'd worked so hard to relegate them to the past.
On reflection, I can see that conflict has been at the heart of each

of my breakdowns. All the ingredients which were to flatten me for a full eight months later on in my career, were there then. I was working really hard, as many hours as I could. On top of that I had a young family to look after (anyone who's been there will tell you how tough that can be). Having children doesn't bring parents closer together; you've got to be strong enough not to get driven apart! In addition to this I was doing tons of work at the local church.

So there I was, playing all the roles that I'd imagined went with the perfect life. Managing a power tools shop. Tick. A decent job with a company car. Tick. Our own house and good money. Tick. We had all the trappings of success. We'd go out to dinner parties with our friends at the church. I should have been really happy about everything, but I wasn't. I'd try to put a brave face on it, but the pressure was becoming overwhelming.

In the end, I was trying to do too much, burning the candle at both ends. Eventually I cracked. I'd work ever harder to meet targets that I knew were beyond the powers of any mortal. In a pattern that would repeat itself, my body just shut down. I had my first breakdown. The GP signed me off for a while. I was on antidepressants for a couple of months, which probably didn't help my profound exhaustion; I had about three months off in total. My doctor was very good. He insisted that I rested and that I should return to work only when I was ready. I worked on getting myself back together, without really thinking about what had put me in the situation in the first place – less the bullying itself than my reaction to it.

Getting so ill was a shock because I'd always been quite fit and healthy. I'd worked hard and made a difference for the guys at the tool hire company. Now I felt that I wasn't wanted and I was unable to stand the level of conflict that that one man had created. He was not a nice man, he didn't have any real empathy at all, and he seemed to get a kick out of being cruel to people.

I'd pushed myself harder and harder to satisfy him, but it was never going to be enough. In the end I had burnt myself out.

Eventually I got myself back together, more through the love of family and friends, and the assistance of prescription pills, than addressing the underlying problems. The firm was great to me while I was going through this, and they never held it against me. They knew I was a good employee, and after I'd been back about a month and a half they promoted me to general manager of a new division, Events and Site Services.

This involved a lot more responsibility, managing site services, looking after hiring kit to outdoor events and traffic management schemes. Talk about work pressure! I had now taken on buying and selling the company's products in a completely new business line. There was a massive team to run since we worked at some pretty big events: Roundhaye Park in Leeds and the county shows. It was getting so complex trying to organise all these activities that I had to learn some more project management skills and eventually became a qualified project manager. By then I was part of the senior management team.

It was a flattering confirmation of how far I'd come and I really enjoyed it again, but I wanted to do things slightly differently. The company was going through a golden period, growing and growing and growing as we opened more depots. From three depots when I started, they'd got something like twenty by the time I left. I bought in to the ambitions of the company. When I was a salesman, I loved being top of my game. When I ran the shop, it had to be super-competitive, a tight ship that made profit; it had to be run right. Every step of the way, the owners helped me and encouraged me and moulded me to do those things. When I was general manager of events and site services, that same ethos carried on. At every turn, I put in more and more hours; I wanted to because I felt the reason I was making a difference was how hard I was working. Each promotion was a new challenge and I grew into it. But, after a period of time, the buzz would go. That sense of dissatisfaction, that dis-ease as I call it, would come seeping back in. In my heart of hearts I knew I wasn't fulfilled because I was being called by God. I wanted a bit more time to devote to preparing for ministry really and a bit more time with my family.

Sudden changes in the company meant one morning I was called into the office and was made redundant. Although it was shattering news and the way it was done was brutal, it gave me an opportunity to look for a new challenge - once I'd got over the shock, that is.

Because I'd been in the industry a long time many people in the region knew me. I got a job with a local company called Derby Industrial Power Tools (DIPT). They were more of a sales company than a hire company and now they wanted to increase their share of the tool hire market. They were looking for someone to be what was called a 'Segment Leader' for their tool hire division across all their branches. They were a very professional outfit. The business was the Marks & Spencer of tool hire and sales in the East Midlands. In the main they dealt with top end industrial companies: in Derby it was Rolls Royce. In Nottingham it was Boots, Players Cigarettes and Central TV. All blue chip outfits. My role was to develop a hire business. So that's what I did.

After the trauma of that first breakdown whilst at the tool hire company , I enjoyed life at DIPT. I had a lot of respect for the managing director, and he was great to work for in return. But I still felt called to do more in the life of the church. It was during my time there that I became a candidate for Methodist ministry and was accepted. The next phase of 'The Plan', which had been on hold ever since those lay worker days, could finally begin in earnest. During my interview the MD had said that DIPT was run on Christian principles. For instance, everyone got decent pay from the cleaner up – this was long before the minimum wage was a political issue. So I knew I could go to The MD about my desire to try for ministry. He was supportive all the way, and I was so grateful for that.

During this whole 15-year period, I had a developing idea of conflict and how it affected me. Conflict and criticism I take very personally, more personally than I need to, perhaps. I can see now that it relates back to my early life, which was tough, and in which my parents weren't as supportive as I'd have wanted. There are loads of people in caring professions – nurses are the obvious ones but ministers of religion come into this bracket too – whose personal mental health needs are poorly understood by the public. You can't do the job without being sensitive and empathetic but that makes you vulnerable to criticism and conflict. Humans can only take so much of it and retain that connection with other people. In my case, I blew up the boiler the first time around. At other times it manifested itself in full-blown depression. Either way, your resilience can eventually be broken down by the demands of others and constant spending of your emotional resources.

In order to deal with the disappointments I felt around my lay ministry and in my work life, I had to develop better coping skills. Some of these were found in prayer and in the Bible. Ideas of forgiveness and healing are crucial, and the work I did with Wholeness Through Christ made a huge difference. On a practical level I found it was a matter of detaching myself from the situation, disengaging from it and almost walking away. This may not be the best method in terms of solving the problem, I am aware of that. But as a minister, you can't burn bridges (much as you might like to) by changing potential conflict into confrontation. As often as not, the people you are in conflict with are around you every day, and may be vital in keeping the church going. You may be dealing with parishioners, with the vulnerable and needy or perhaps with people who are members of a committee or management team. These are the awkward circumstances you are often placed in. You have to avoid making the conflict worse, no matter how irritated you are or how unjustly you feel you are treated.

Looking back, I can see that the transformation and growth was in that land between those two places. Leaving Cliff with all its subsequent disappointments and realising I was still so angry from being a kid. Being a family man, growing with Alison and David and getting used to all that. Growing as a Christian and thinking about service and ministry and training. Then I grew in my career, but it never truly gave satisfaction, and made me seriously ill for a period.

More recently, I've realised you don't have to take all the confrontation, criticism and bullying personally. Other people's behaviour is a product of their circumstances, which will be different from yours. You have to allow for others' weaknesses as you allow for your own. With that knowledge I can pray for forgiveness and understanding for myself. I can pray that relationships stay whole and that where there is disunity, harmony can be restored. If people are making personal attacks on you it is because they feel vulnerable. Any form of change makes human beings feel vulnerable which in turn leads to fear and conflict. The real question, which we'll come back to later, is how to offer people a way out of conflict so they can retain their dignity.

But first, I'd like to take you through both the most exciting and most depressing phases of my career. These phases followed each other in short order, and were the unexpected consequence of coming into my calling – that of becoming an ordained Diaconal minister in the Methodist church.

Chapter Five

Training at Queens College and Ministry in Hull

So Christ himself gave the apostles, the prophets, the evangelists, the pastors and teachers. Ephesians 4:11 NIV

I was now taking up my vocation. I'd known it was what I'd been called to ever since those days in Tipton Street. Even when I was on my knees weeping over my past I longed for the transformed life I saw ahead of me. I was pretty sure I could leave my troubles behind me - those episodes of depression and burnout. I'd been dragged through those periods by my friends and family, but in all honesty, I'd not really stopped and looked inside myself. I'd not really thought about what the real problem was. Now, this didn't matter for a while, as I was so excited to be engaged, finally, in my true vocation. If I thought about it all, I think I assumed that everything was going to be fine from now on – in the bosom of the church, with a loving community around me.

Spoiler alert! Things didn't change.

I was shocked by the way some people in the life of the church treated each other. In a way that no one can describe as Christian. Sometimes it seems that we have forgotten how to love our neighbours, to treat each other with respect, and to separate the public from the private.

I left the tool hire firm with the CEO's blessing on the Friday and went to Queens College in Birmingham on the Wednesday. I had such a great time at Queens. We were exposed to so many good things: broad teaching, good colleagues, good staff. All in all it was a really positive experience. It broadened me theologically and as a person. There were Methodists, Anglicans, and students from the United Reformed Church. We also did a four week module with the Roman Catholics. We lived in their college (Oscott) for two weeks and they lived with us at Queens for two weeks. It was part of the ethos of the college to promote debate between denominations and encourage scholarship.

The Bachelor of Arts course in Applied Theology was quite practical, and we had to do some placements. I did an attachment with the TUC, at an urban priority primary school, and with the industrial mission team in Birmingham. This was new to me, this chaplaincy, but it was great to be exposed to it in so many different contexts. After each placement you'd reflect on your experience from a theological perspective. We covered a lot of what you'd expect, for example, Old Testament, New Testament, Christian History, Pastoral Care and Ethics. As a diaconal student, you engage with the same material as a Presbyterial student.

I'd read widely by the time I started – it was twenty years and more since my experiences at Tipton Street. Since then I'd done loads of training and been on as many courses as I could. I'd had some experience of preaching and leading groups. And of course I went as a mature student. I felt as though the timing was right for me to be in that place. I was more organised than one or two of the younger ones; that's one of the advantages of being a bit older. This came in handy as it turns out you have to be pretty organised to get through a BA in two years. There's no let up, and you always have extra work to do.

While I was going up to Birmingham, Alison and David carried on living in Derby. Some people might think I had the best of both worlds for a couple of years. Student life with all that brings but family as well. On the other hand, it was quite lonely at times, especially night times studying in my bedroom, in the college accommodation, in the middle of Birmingham. Each weekend I drove home, as it was less than an hour each way. Back home it was great to be with my family. I kept in touch with the local church and would preach from time to time as part of the college plan. When there were placements I didn't have to go back to college much, which meant I got to see my family a bit more often.

Following God's call often requires sacrifice. For us this sacrifice made itself felt in the lack of money and the restriction on our time together as a family. And yet, God is good. I can honestly say that this was one of the most positive periods of my life. It was a healing time. I felt I was really in the right place. It was liberating to be with like-minded people who were hungry for scripture and learning and who wanted to serve God as ministers in His Church. I enjoyed the entire course - there was nothing I didn't like. The whole experience was new; obviously I didn't go to University when I was younger, I started out with no qualifications. That whole experience of student life was a precious gift. It was totally the right decision. I found everything to be positive and exciting. I had no anchoring, no cynicism. The contrast with tool hire couldn't have been starker. It was important to me to get that underpinning and that understanding of what ministry was about.

While training at Queens and later as a probationary Deacon I went through assessments. The idea is that when you leave college you do two years as a 'probationary minister'. The technical term for a probationary minister in the Methodist Church is a 'theologically educated lay person' as you're not ordained at that stage. So you go through different committees and assessments. Reports are written by the college which are then sent back to the Methodist Church. Hopefully the church says, 'Yes we'll continue to support you as you prepare for ministry.' Then you're into the second year and you enter into the process to determine where it is you'll serve.

After two intense years (instead of the normal three), I passed my BA in Applied Theology and I achieved a 2:1. Not bad for a Black Country lad who left school with no qualifications! I was chuffed, not half. A few weeks later, we had our graduation ceremony, and I didn't mind dressing up for an afternoon. I felt as though I was reasonably well-equipped to start my ministry as a probationary deacon.

What a journey. When I reflected on it, to start with nothing and to come so far. To have the love and support of my family. To be able to fulfil my vocation. It seemed almost dreamlike that it could all be happening. That's why I was so content at college and for some time afterwards; I was in a place of consolation and looking forward to ministry.

When you're at the end your time at College the senior Methodist tutor at the college gets all the presbyter and deacon students together in a room. It's like something out of a reality TV show. That's when you're told where you're going. Sometime earlier you'd have filled in a profile and a form with your personal details and what type of ministry you might be able to offer and so on. We were quite open about where we wanted to go, Alison and I. We wanted the right appointment, and so we were asked to go to East Hull. We went and had a look at the place. You don't have to accept the appointment, but you'd better find a very good reason not to, especially as a probationer. You couldn't complain about the colour of the curtains in the manse for instance. But we took a look, and the job seemed ideal, really. It fitted in with my ideas of mission and outreach and evangelism, and Alison was totally on board, so we upped sticks and headed east. I remember feeling a sense of guilt that David was having to leave his school and all the friends he'd made there, but again we knew we had no other choice than to trust God.

East Hull's a pretty tough place - you wouldn't necessarily want to go there on your holidays but there were plenty of really good people to be found. I was there for over six years and looking back on it now, they were six good years. I enjoyed the job a lot, and I learnt a lot, it was very fruitful. In that ministry, with the help of the local community, we had some great results. I was responsible for demolishing and rebuilding a church. This was on a post-war council estate called Bilton Grange. The Methodist church in the 50s had bought an acre of land there and built this big huge citadel of a building that dwarfed the estate. That church had since fallen into disrepair – there had been arson and all sorts. So eventually there was this tiny, ageing congregation and no real engagement with the community on the estate. The pastoral issue was that the building was just a drain, so we explored some ideas about what we might do with this building[1].

To cut a long story short, it was in the days when there was a lot of Sure Start money around. Sure Start was part of Tony Blair's 'Education, education, education' project and it was to do with preschool and the foundation years. The ideas originated in America where there's good evidence that the cycle of deprivation and underachievement can be broken by intervention in the preschool years. Gordon Brown was behind bringing these ideas over to this country. So there was that money from the government, but there was a lot of European money too, from the ERDF - the European Regional Development Fund, especially for urban priority areas like East Hull. And there was

---

1 See apendix 1a

a lottery scheme running in tandem called the Neighbourhood Nursery Fund. I got a team of people together and we were able to apply for those big grants. We were successful in nearly all of them. We did some really good research into community needs in the area, plus we had a supportive local MP, John Prescott. We raised about £3 million altogether. The Methodist church donated the land in lieu of cash to kick start this scheme. It was enough to pull in more funding. The church also gave my time to project manage it and pull the whole thing together. You can see some more details on the Imagine website[2] if you're interested.

So we put a number of different projects into this place, all based on our research and community needs. There was a job centre, a nursery, a youth centre and the chapel itself, which could also be used as meeting rooms. There was a children's centre and a community café, all coming together as 'The Acorns'. I reckon it's a model for how the church should reach out into the community, meet people where they are and welcome everyone into Christian life by acts of meaningful service[3].

The neighbourhood nursery was funded separately as a business and run by a private provider. This helped to make the project sustainable financially, as there was an income stream after all the capital spending. This was where all the commercial project and business management I had done suddenly found a different outlet. It wasn't how I expected things to go, it had nothing to do with two years at college, more to do with a practical need on the ground, but I seemed to have the right skills in the right place at the right time.

During your time on probation you undertake some form of study. I completed a Masters Degree in Evangelism Studies at

---

2 www.imagineprojects.co.uk

3 See Appendix 1b

Cliff College. When my 2 years' probation had come to an end I was ordained. This happened in Llandudno, which was where the Methodist Conference was held that year. We all processed on the stage in front of everyone, and then we went off to our services to be ordained. It was great, it meant a lot to me and Alison; it was a real watershed moment. It showed we'd come to the end of one long journey, although our next journey into full time ministry was already well underway. I went off to Llandudno as a probationer and came back Deacon Ian.

I was also involved in another church further up the road called Kingston Wesley. Again there was this big building with quite an elderly congregation. There were, however some lively, younger families and I did the all-age worship parade services every month. I put on holiday clubs and family fun days. Out of that the Maximum Life Youth Project was born[4]. That was work which was also built from the bottom up. We set up a separate charity and were successful with funding applications from Children in Need and the Church Urban Fund and Tudor Trust. Then we were able to employ a full time youth development worker. We set up all sorts there: a recording studio, theatre, arts, film and so on. It was very family orientated, so again, going from an elderly Sunday morning congregation to a thriving family-focused place was transformational for the life of the church. More importantly it was transformational for the people who came to use our services.

I was able to engage with other aspects of ministry in Hull. I was truly blessed by the chaplaincy at Prince's Quay shopping centre one morning a week; that was a pastoral role. I loved it. I used to walk round and 'loiter with intent'. It was great to go into the shops and just chat. Some people were glad to see you and of course some weren't. We put on events on occasions like

---

[4] See Appendix 2

September 11th and Remembrance Day. We always did things at Christmas and Easter. Sometimes I had my dog collar on, but I've never been a great lover of that stuff. It's a bit of a double-edged sword; it can either be off-putting or help make you identifiable. I'd just rather have a badge that said 'Chaplain' on it, because otherwise people would run and hide, or be on their best behaviour. 'Don't swear' is the one I'd always hear whispered as I walked into a shop. They didn't know my background in Dudley! I've heard more swearing than they would ever have done. Years in tool hire makes you pretty immune to most stuff. At Princes Quay I felt like part of the team. Staff there would tell me about folks who needed support.

There was also a wider city mission called 'There Is Hope' with a wonderful gentleman called David Hill. We organised events around and about to give people hope in a city where there wasn't much hope to be had. We put on Easter Praise at City Hall; it was a great blessing. Weddings seemed to become my speciality. I did an awful lot of weddings at Kingston Wesley. It was such a lovely place and people wanted to come and get hitched there. One couple stick out in my mind, Nigel and Tracy, who ran the Four in Hand pub. We became really good friends and they let me put on a Christian ministry in the pub on a Tuesday night, once a month, called 'Something To Declare at the Four In Hand'. This was before the smoking ban so we always seemed to sit in this big fog, with the dockers coming off the wharves and sparking up their cigarettes and necking their pints. It was a raw ministry really, but I loved it. We sustained that night for about three years. I got on really well with that family. I married Nigel and Tracy, but I also did the funerals for their parents, christenings for their kids, everything.

In the end we spent six years there, in Hull, but eventually the time came to move on. I felt I'd had a really good ministry, made a difference in people's lives and had put the church in a position to grow and reach out to people in their communities. Now it was time to do something different, and after the usual form-filling and so on, we were offered a ministry in Lowestoft in Suffolk. This was a change – we'd be a long way from David (now 31 and a Broadcast Technician with the BBC) and our families, particularly Alison's. Lowestoft was a rural parish with a massive new dormitory housing development being built alongside it. We expected challenges, but we had no idea of what actually lay ahead of us.

Chapter Six

Opposition to the Building: Carlton Colville

"And it came to pass, that when all our enemies heard thereof, and all the heathen that were about us saw these things, they were much cast down in their own eyes: for they perceived that this work was wrought of our God." Nehemiah 6:16-17

I recall my spiritual director in Hull saying to me once that, as a minister, I would be vulnerable. I don't think I fully appreciated what she was saying at the time but my ministry in Carlton Colville, Lowestoft, taught me something of the nature of ministry that would shape my own in terms of community, creativity, change, conflict and criticism.

Nehemiah illustrates the challenge of ministry perfectly. With his team he rebuilds the walls of Jerusalem, brick by brick and meets with the challenge of resistance and opposition as he does so. Sanballet bullies, undermines and generally makes life difficult for Nehemiah and his team.

In Nehemiah 4:1&2 we read, "When Sanballat heard that we were rebuilding the walls of Jerusalem, he was very angry and upset. He started making fun of the Jews. Sanballat talked with his friends and the army at Samaria and said, "What are these weak Jews doing? Do they think we will leave them alone? Do they think they will offer sacrifices? Maybe they think they can finish building in only one day. They cannot bring stones back to life from these piles of trash and dirt. These are just piles of ashes and dirt!"

And yet, brick by brick, the wall was re-built, heralding the return of thousands of exiles.

The story of Nehemiah also illustrates how creative ministry can be and how change, conflict and criticism are interwoven and form the same thread. It shows how blessed we are if we are part of a vibrant Christian community.

We were to serve in a new and exciting project in Carlton Colville, a suburb of Lowestoft, near to the Norfolk Broads in beautiful Suffolk. Around the original village were thousands of new houses which spread for several miles. My brief was to care for the current congregation, pioneer new ways of working and help form community through fresh expressions of church. The wider Methodist Church viewed Carlton Colville as a mission opportunity and a harvest field where the Church could learn valuable lessons that could be applied to other areas of new housing. The expectation locally was that I would lead the small, traditional and mainly elderly congregation in to renewal.

One of the challenges that was clear to me was that there was a disconnection between the local church and the needs of the community on the new estates around it. We needed to be creative in in our approach. The vision I presented to my management committee and the Church Council was to engage in a community survey. For me this was a logical thing to do, a hangover from work. Every time we were thinking of opening a new shop we'd carry out some local research to understand the local economy. In doing so we would have an informed view of the type of tools and accessories we should stock. We'd judge the demand for different products and build our business case on the back of that. Why would we not do the same when beginning a new ministry from a local Church and get a feel for the needs of the local community? So we set to work building, section by section as we connected with the local community through the survey, engaging in mission as we did so. I have yet to do a community survey with a local church and not be surprised at the outcomes. There is always something unexpected, surprising and exciting. Something on which to build a Christian ministry and mission, one brick at a time.

I wanted to try and find out what the community wanted rather than what I thought they wanted. The overwhelming response through the survey was for health and fitness opportunities, a community cinema and activities for young families. The next step was to ask the children and young people themselves whether they wanted to have such provision.

This research was carried out by groups from within the schools themselves while Christian Research did all the analysis. It mirrored our first research results and also told us what children and young people meant by 'activities'. What they really wanted was a good place to chill out and relax, somewhere they could go to be with their friends, play with their PlayStations and Wii gaming machines.

As health and fitness seemed so popular among local people the steering group I set up decided to further explore the relationship between faith and fitness. I also decided to embark on a feasibility study for a new building because of the evidence in the research. The work we were doing was developing nicely, both in the church building and in the local schools and community centres. We appointed Momentum Business Developments as our consultants, the Leisure Database Company, to provide us with data, analysis and advice for a financially sustainable fitness centre. A sport and leisure trust called Active Luton also acted as our consultants and Westray Keith Phelps Ltd as architects. The project became known as the Discovery Family Centre and was just so exciting. However, not all projects reach completion for many reasons. We completed the design phase along with a profesional businessplan. And then it had to stop. It was very disapointing but these things happen.[5]

Cre8 came about as a result of the research. I got together a small team to get things off the ground, including someone who worked with the Schools Partnership Agency. As we had a professional musician in the team, we started with children and young people taking part in shows. Their parents would come along with them on Saturday mornings for rehearsals and have a bite of breakfast with us. At that time the Christian input was very small because we were at the stage of simply wanting to build relationships with the children and their parents. It was, however, during this inception stage that we began to see the development of a holistic ministry, that is a ministry in which Christian spirituality is very much seen as part of a person's physical, social, mental and emotional health and wellbeing.

The spiritual dimension is always present because of our desire for God to be at the heart of it all, involved in every aspect of the project, and because we know that all glory must be His. This was expressed in the project's ten core values. I believe that values are important to any project as they become the road map that guides people on the journey. The values this particular project adopted were: We live, We influence, We celebrate, We transform, We give, We include, We create, We learn, We pray and We worship. Our mission statement was quite simply "To build lives and build community". A local school produced a logo which expressed the core values and the

---

[5] Appendix 3 shows the building design and health and fitness suites.

mission statement.
As all this work was building up into something solid; congregations at Sunday morning services were also growing, especially at the monthly family service. For example, on Father's Day the service was aimed at blokes – we enjoyed bacon sandwiches, a Yorkie bar challenge, a clip from a Rob Bell DVD and a lot of bunting and a banner made by the kids! We also had very low-key Communion with them. At one such Communion, we looked at the meaning of symbols. We started off looking at McDonald's, Nike and KFC. What did their 'symbols', their logos, say about them? We then moved on to the symbolic meaning of the bread and wine. It was all consecrated properly but we served the wine in paper cups and gave sliced bread. It was all familiar to them.
Fridays@7 was another development, a predominantly male, café church environment where people could chill out, eat, drink coffee, watch films, enjoy music and explore what faith in Jesus is all about. It's amazing what has happened there. One guy loves Shakespeare and he went out to buy himself a King James Bible because he sees parallels between the two; there were a lot of programmes on radio and TV at the time about the King James' 400th anniversary and he was fascinated by it. From time to time we'd meet at a local pub. We called this evening 'Who Let the Dads Out?'. We went go karting, walking, and other fun things that men enjoy and we encouraged our non-church friends to join us on these occasions. Soon, the various activities started to flow into each other, for example two of the guys from Fridays@7 also led the gardening club at Cre8. We ran events for families in the community which were always well supported. We also created two jobs for local people – a part time administrator and a year's part time gap-year post. In all of this, there were struggles and it didn't come together easily. It was certainly a painful process at times. Leading three

congregations was a challenge so we needed to be creative with our model of leadership. We tried to facilitate communication between the inherited church and the Fresh Expressions of church. We'd meet once a quarter with representatives from the different areas of church life to plan and discuss. The Fresh Expressions group was always very firm in saying that it was as much their church as it was the inherited church but they also knew that it is all about working together for the good of the Kingdom. This is not always an easy journey. However the fruit was so good. Over a period of a few years a conservative and traditional Sunday morning congregation had turned into a mixed economy of vibrant congregations. We were working towards a rich sense of unity and diversity.

We needed a creative method of leadership that would enable the church as a whole to continue to grow numerically and spiritually and produce leaders that would allow the mission and ministry of the church to be sustained.

Ephesians 4:11[6] presents a leadership framework that embraces unity and diversity and encourages growth. It seemed that the inherited church were comfortable with a traditional model of leadership that had a preference for hierarchical structure which favoured a chain of command approach with a focus on pastoral care and teaching.

In a creative mission-focused church the Ephesians 4 model includes pastoral care and teaching and adds three other leadership functions; Apostle, Prophet and Evangelist.

- The Apostle encourages pioneering activity and oversees its development.

---

[6] "So Christ himself gave the apostles, the prophets, the evangelists, the pastors and teachers"

- Prophecy seeks to discern the spiritual realities in a situation and communicate them.

- Evangelism seeks to communicate the gospel of Jesus in such a way that people can respond in faith and grow as Christians.

Teaching communicates the revealed wisdom of God so people can develop in their faith.

- Pastoral care is the glue that holds every thing together.

This model creates a flat model of leadership that allows for great diversity within a context of an even deeper, underlying unity.

With the rich diversity of mission and ministry that was developing at Carlton this model worked well, despite the on-going tension that existed from some sectors of the inherited congregation.

Because, as always, the Sanballats of this world were never far away, criticizing and causing unrest. It's a very normal thing for all of us to fear change. I'd seen it in my previous work life and other church congregations. The idea of change is welcomed until it actually arrives. No one knows where the changes will manifest themselves, what form the changes will take and who will be affected by them. How many of us pray for change and renewal and then feel uncomfortable and frightened when our prayers are answered in ways we hadn't expected or wanted? Change and conflict are two sides of the same coin.

I am sure that many leaders and pioneers reading this book will have experienced conflict that arises during change and how devastating to people it can be. The distress, discomfort, pain and anger can become the focus of your thoughts and energy. Rumination is not good and the enemy loves it. Because my

default position was to push myself and work harder and harder and because my thought patterns were so negative, I was heading straight for a second melt down.
It's interesting to look at Nehemiah chapter 4 and see how he responds to the opposition he comes up against. I'm struck by the fact that he prays (Nehemiah 4:4 & 9) and then supports, protects and equips his team to do the work:

"Hear us, our God, for we are despised. Turn their insults back on their own heads. Give them over as plunder in a land of captivity. Do not cover up their guilt or blot out their sins from your sight, for they have thrown insults in the face of the builders.
So we rebuilt the wall till all of it reached half its height, for the people worked with all their heart.
But when Sanballat, Tobiah, the Arabs, the Ammonites and the people of Ashdod heard that the repairs to Jerusalem's walls had gone ahead and that the gaps were being closed, they were very angry. They all plotted together to come and fight against Jerusalem and stir up trouble against it. But we prayed to our God and posted a guard day and night to meet this threat."

Nehemiah and his team worked alongside one another, and watching over each other, safe in the knowledge that God was with them and would fight for them (4:20). I just wasn't very well equipped to deal with the conflict. It seemed I was building and defending single-handedly. My fear of failure and need to be needed took over as I worked ever harder. My disappointment was absolute, that calling I had sensed for years ringing in my ears.
During this time, I received the blessing of a three month sabbatical, granted for length of service. This was a true gift of space and time.
For four weeks Alison and I travelled to the United States to

visit churches with health and fitness as an expression of their ministry. It was a wonderful trip. But this was to be a short-lived relief. Just three days before I was due back to work, I was called into a meeting that would finally plunge me into a second meltdown this would change my life and ministry forever. It was a water shed moment, a massive turning point in my life.

Reflecting on this pivotal moment in my life I recall the story of the stoning of Stephen in Acts chapter 7:

"At this they covered their ears and, yelling at the top of their voices, they all rushed at him, dragged him out of the city and began to stone him. Meanwhile, the witnesses laid their coats at the feet of a young man named Saul." Acts 7:57-59.

The stoning of Stephen was a watershed moment in the story of the expansion of the Gospel. The fall out from this event is recorded in Acts 8 as the church is persecuted and Christians are scattered throughout Judea and Samaria. In a similar way, my watershed moment in Carlton Colville led to a hunger for a deeper understanding of myself and Christian spirituality. On return from my sabbatical, I experienced the biggest and most unprofessional grilling I'd ever had. It felt like my own personal stoning. After the interview, I began to think that I couldn't encourage good people to be part of something if their lives might be as damaged as mine was now. I did wonder if I could carry on encouraging people to come to Jesus, encouraging people to express that within the church I had loved and served as a lay and ordained person for over thirty years.

After that terrible meeting I went downhill rapidly. Within a couple of weeks I was signed off work with depression. I was totally run down and I found it really difficult to cope with the things which were happening around me. My body just shut down. All I wanted to do was shut the door and lock my self away. It was better for me to keep my head down, lie on the sofa with the dog at my feet and just think, 'Leave me alone, I can't be bothered.'

I'm pleased to say that I didn't get to the point where I wanted to end my life, for me it never got that grim. It did get bad enough though that I couldn't cope and I just wanted to be alone. During that time I prayed every day for encouragement and each day I received my answer through a deep sense of peace.

As my family says, I didn't do anything to warrant the sort of abuse and bullying that I'd been subjected to. It wasn't really about me at all and yet it was all about me. It was about me in as much as conflict had reared its ugly head again; it was personal and yet that conflict was never really about me as a person. When the walls start to take shape, the conflict begins. Unlike Nehemiah, I felt unprotected and ill equipped to deal with it. Unlike Nehemiah I couldn't delegate and so I worked ever harder always pushing to achieve. Nehemiah completed the wall and thousands of captives were blessed. One of my reports to the management committee made the following observation about the work we had done:

"Our story is that it is possible to change an inherited, maintenance-minded, traditional congregation into a mission shaped model, giving birth to a mixed economy of congregations in a small building."

When I look back at my ministry in Carlton Colville, as I often do, I see a time of great Kingdom productivity. It was really incredible to see what God did in that place. I also look at that time and see a perfect illustration of all the lessons I would need to learn. That was the place where I was broken but I see now that it was in that same dark place where the healing started. God still uses that watershed moment to speak and minister to

me and He is still directing my steps through it today.
Back then though, I knew it was time to move on. I knew I needed a new appointment closer to home and to my family. My third appointment was in York. I was to serve in a team across three Methodist churches. It seemed ideal and I was thrilled to be taking up another mission role with so many prospects.

Chapter Seven

Ministry in York - Going Outside of the Church

"During the night Paul had a vision of a man of Macedonia standing and begging him, "Come over to Macedonia and help us." After Paul had seen the vision, we got ready at once to leave for Macedonia, concluding that God had called us to preach the gospel to them." Acts 16:9-11

So we were on our way to York! We found the city really well connected by road and rail; it seemed like an ideal place for us. We were near our son and his family, some of Alison's family were just down the road in Derby and I could get to my parents without too much trouble. We were also back in our comfort zone: steel and concrete around us and masses of people everywhere.

That was 2012 and we're still here. The ride hasn't been easy, interrupted by two meltdowns in four years. In writing this book, I've had to think carefully about the threads that weave their way through my story: community, challenge, creativity, change, conflict and criticism. I am aware that I am motivated by a deep desire to bring about new life, growth and change. There doesn't seem to be much wrong with that and yet, I have watched myself overwork and overcommit my way into vulnerable positions. It is almost as if I've been addicted to work as a means of self-expression. By that I mean that I keep seeking out work, I can't get enough of it; it's like a drug to me, where the hit is in self-worth and self-esteem. But the reason I know I'm an addict is that it makes me ill again and again, and yet I keep going back to it. It damages me and it damages my family. Whilst I know my deepest motivations are sound, it's really hard trying to break the vicious cycle of work, over-work and illness. It's very much one day at a time. The key thing has been to recognise my illness for what it is, and to start to deal with some of the issues around self-esteem that have blighted me. Let me tell you how being in York has helped because of the interventions of a number of key people who have nudged me onto the road to being whole.

When we first arrived, I worked in three churches, Acomb, Lidgett Gove and Copmanthorpe. I was part of a team. As before, I commissioned a survey for each church. Each survey created fantastic opportunities and none more so than at Lidgett Grove. The church building here was large and falling into disrepair and the congregation in the main was elderly and traditional. The Joseph Rowntree Foundation had recently completed a piece of work exploring neighbourhood approaches to loneliness on a local Estate named Carr. We picked up on the Joseph Rowntree work and carried it forward through the community survey. The survey shone a light on a lack of meeting places for local people which was contributing towards a sense of isolation and loneliness. The fruits are there for all to see with a resurgence in the use of building: a sustainable community café that has eighty people meeting together every Wednesday morning, a messy church that meets each month. We even created a part time administration role for a local person to manage booking enquiries and suchlike.

One of the major emphases placed on Diaconal ministry is that it should take the church beyond its walls into the community and bring the community into the church forming those links. In York, we'd opened up avenues for fresh expressions of ministry and mission. We'd encourage new people into the church. However as soon as new people join anything the dynamics change and the potential for conflict arises. This is not just my experience; it's part of the bigger picture, the context in which the church is operating. A phrase that is frequently used when discussing the current cultural context is post-modernity. This period of history outlines the fragmentation of modernism, which was defined by grand narratives or universal truths, for example; Marxism, Capitalism, Fascism, National Socialism and Western Christianity. Stanley Grenz, a leading evangelical scholar, says in his book A Primer on Postmodernism, 'the demise of the grand narrative means we no longer search for the one system of myths that can unite human beings into one people, or the globe into one world' (Grenz, 1966). We live in changing, fragmented, confused times, as Dr. Harry Lee Poe adds, 'the post-modern generation will not visit the church building. They will not go to a lecture. They will not join the organisation. The church looks like one more institution. They're not interested in institutions, but in relationships. We have to go to them for them to listen to us, the sharing of the gospel has to take place in a relational way, that is a conversation' (Lee Poe, 2001).

The catalyst for effective mission therefore, is our ability to listen to people's life stories in all their richness and variety. People enjoy stories and they relate to them. Listening to others' stories builds relationships. Jesus himself taught and built relationships using the story as a vehicle for his message. Relationships are important; they provide a sense of belonging, inspired by confidence and trust. Finney states, in Recovering the Past, 'the importance of an open community with integrity is obvious when the results of research are taken into account.

Finding faith today shows that most people come to faith through relationships' (Finney, 1998). An effective strategic plan for mission and ministry must therefore take the importance of relationships into account.

And that's it in a nutshell; that's what we were trying to do, have a conversation. Yet the reality of the approach is uncomfortable for some people within the church to engage with. There can be a chasm between what people outside the church need and what some churches can offer.

In York like on so many other occasions I found myself in a situation in which the level of conflict was sky-high and the demands I was putting on myself were mounting rapidly. It broke me. I found I was the instigator of a lot of the change - that's why I took the criticism personally. People say, 'Don't take it personally', but you can't always help it. Some of the emails I had, some of the phone calls, were awful. At one Church I felt as though I needed to wear a hard hat when I went in. I wondered what the next avalanche was going to be, where the next bit of grief was to come from. It crossed the line of what I felt was acceptable. Again, I started to have major questions about encouraging good people who were searching for something in their life. These were people we'd met exactly where they were, we'd engaged with them. They were hungry but I feared they could be damaged by being part of the church. This may sound unfair but its how I felt.

I love the church. Let me say that straight away. I don't like a lot of the behaviour I've encountered but I still hold a deep desire to serve and to see the Church serve the people around it. My core belief is that the church should be a healing place where the broken can come and find a safe place to fall. My vision for the church is that it should be an A&E for those who need healing, who need love, who need hope, who need the Saviour. The Church and those serving within and alongside it could provide a space for mental, emotional, physical, spiritual and social healing. The local church and its people should be equipped, enabled and encouraged to help people reach their God given potential.

In my thirty plus years of experience working with churches and community groups, in a variety of situations, both as a lay person and as an ordained Methodist Deacon, I have enabled groups to effectively engage with contemporary culture. The three main reactions I have encountered whilst working with such groups are as follows:

Tired and inflexible – some churches and groups are tired and firmly set in their ways. In some cases they have disconnected themselves from the communities they once served. They have unintentionally pulled up a drawbridge, locked themselves in and the community out. Their focus is on 'their' church, 'their' meetings and 'their' very traditional Sunday Morning Services. Therefore the majority of people in the surrounding community are left outside; they perceive what happens inside to be dry and uninspiring. Sadly the practices of this particular kind of church are stuck in a rut. One influential Methodist Minister once said, 'the only difference between a rut and a grave is its depth'. Consequently any form of change is, at best, frowned upon and, at worst, fought against. The key phrase is 'over my dead body will they do that here'. Such an attitude can be bruising for a leader who wishes to instigate change and attempt to slightly lower the drawbridge, to let people in so that they can see the fantastic time that can be had when you belong to a local church and experience faith in Christ.

Enthusiastic but in need of direction – some churches are keen to engage with their local community and simply need some help to get started.

Enthusiastic and energetic – some churches are fortunate, they overflow with enthusiasm and energy. However there may be a tendency to launch into strategies, ideas and 'how to' questions without first without addressing the cultural context in which they are set.

In Great Britain today the church is faced with new challenges to belief and mission. These challenges bring with them exciting opportunities, opportunities not dissimilar to those faced by the early Church. If you can, take a moment to read the Acts of the Apostles. It highlights the pluralist, multicultural context in which the gospel was first introduced but it also tells of a group of men and women who dared to dream. They had an impossible vision that they refused to give up on. We live in a society today, which for the first time in many generations, has little or no knowledge of Christianity. Today's climate has many parallels with that in which the early church was being built. It was a time of huge opportunity set against a backdrop of impossible dreams.

In York, for example, the ministry at Copmanthorpe was different in that it was more about spiritual development and encouraging people who were already on fire for God to look outwards. The community survey helped with that. As always, the survey highlighted some particular issues specific to Copmanthorpe, an affluent area with no apparent social deprivation. However once we scratched beneath the surface a little we found there was hidden deprivation. In Copmanthorpe loneliness is prevalent, mainly because there are many single parents, older people and a culture of working long hours. This sense of loneliness was felt across all age groups.

At Acomb we discovered issues unique to that context and a Presbyter colleague of mine took the lead on following that work up. So you see, there were amazing things happening but the volume of work had crept up on me and the conflict was at an all time high.

One evening, Alison and I were watching TV. She could see

I was struggling. The next morning she made me go to the doctor, who prescribed me anti-depressants and wanted me signed off work straight away for two weeks. I reluctantly agreed but found it really hard to stop. I started dipping back in a little bit, and pretty soon afterwards I collapsed with exhaustion. My doctor then signed me off work for a whole month which later became eight months. I was so catatonic, I seemed to exist solely to sleep. That work ethic of mine had put me into a corner. Less an ethic perhaps than an unbearable burden. Buckling under this burden, I soon lost myself once more to burnout and depression.

While I was off work, the superintendent minister at the time worked with me to explore my work load, sense of calling and a possible way forward. This care was incredible and enabled me to put things in focus. The upshot was that my role was realigned to be a wider circuit role, like a consultancy, and I would have a support/steering group to manage my activities.

This meant a step away for me from Acomb and Copmanthorpe. My involvement in Lidgett Grove increased and I was commissioned to carry out a piece of work at Shipton On Beningborough.

The congregation at Shipton had dwindled to such a degree that the village church had to close as a place of worship. The Circuit Council agreed not to sell the building but to look at new ways in which it could be used to further the Kingdom of God. We started with a community survey and uncovered some ways in which the building could be used. Creating a base for relational evangelism.

The village had little in the way of amenities. Through the survey our thoughts turned towards a café which had worked at Lidgett Grove. And we explored starting a cinema. Then we thought, 'Wouldn't it be great to have a shop in the village?' The real problem was how to stock it. And it was then that we drew on ideas commonly referred to as new monasticism[7]. We asked ourselves if a community of believers could grow food for sale in the shop. This would really be reaching out to local people. We believed this could be a very holistic way of bringing the building back to life and helping to form community that meets real needs in a Christian context. It's really exciting because this village looked like it was tired from the perspective of Christian worship, but it's been able to come back another way in the spirit of renewal.

I was also commissioned to carry out a community survey in the city centre of York at Central Methodist Church. Centrals story is similar to so many Churches a very big building housing a mainly elderly congregation. The congregation at Central were exploring how their building could be made fit for purpose for current and future generations.

So we conducted a survey and discovered some encouraging opportunities for the building. On completion of the survey I handed over the report for the congregation to use as they saw fit.

Once this piece of work was completed I started to feel myself shut down and I knew then that something needed to change. I was heading for another meltdown; the second in three and a half years. This time the dark times were truly dark, almost to the point of being unbearable. My doctor signed me off for long periods of time and increased my medication. Around this time, I started to meditate once more on 1 Kings19. It had been given to me by Rev Paul Golightly on a retreat I'd been on to St Anthony's during one of my periods of recovery. The story of Elijah's flight to the desert and his subsequent return was transformational for me. As you'll read in the next chapter, it became a vehicle for my healing and renewal. It helped me to

---

7 See Appendix 4

make sense of some of the dark places I'd been to and started me thinking about a new way back.

I knew that, just like the early church in the book of Acts, the context was complicated, the victories hard won but I also knew that the victories were there. I was not willing to give up on the opportunities even if they are set against a backdrop of impossibility.

During my time in York it became apparent that things had to change. I was burnt out and struggling with depression. I began to consider retiring on health grounds. My doctor supported my application to retire, which in turn was accepted by the Methodist Church. Retirement was to be a new stream of healing which was to reshape my life.

Chapter Eight

Streams of Healing in the Desert

The desert and the parched land will be glad; the wilderness will rejoice and blossom. Like the crocus, it will burst into bloom; it will rejoice greatly and shout for joy. The glory of Lebanon will be given to it, the splendour of Carmel and Sharon; they will see the glory of the Lord, the splendour of our God. Strengthen the feeble hands, steady the knees that give way; say to those with fearful hearts, 'Be strong, do not fear; your God will come, he will come with vengeance; with divine retribution he will come to save you.' Then will the eyes of the blind be opened and the ears of the deaf unstopped. Then will the lame leap like a deer, and the mute tongue shout for joy. Water will gush forth in the wilderness and streams in the desert. The burning sand will become a pool, the thirsty ground bubbling springs. In the haunts where jackals once lay, grass and reeds and papyrus will grow. And a highway will be there; it will be called the Way of Holiness; it will be for those who walk on that Way. The unclean will not journey on it; wicked fools will not go about on it. No lion will be there, nor any ravenous beast; they will not be found there. But only the redeemed will walk there, and those the Lord has rescued will return. They will enter Zion with singing, everlasting joy will crown their heads. Gladness and joy will overtake them and sorrow and sighing will flee away.
Isaiah 35, 1-11

Reflecting on my journey, I have recognised a tendency to overcommit and over-work. This tendency is particularly strong if the project leads to change, conflict and criticism. In my life these strands are interwoven and ultimately develop into burnout and depression. What is also interesting is that it seems like I'm getting sensitised to these triggers, a bit like a sufferer of a nut allergy: each exposure hits harder.

That said, God has given me several sources for healing. He has spoken to me through His Word, taught me about prayer and put people in my path who have helped me greatly. God's healing has come to me like streams in the desert, love flowing in dry places with grace and healing. It is my belief that these streams of healing will unwind the damaging threads of the past that have caused me so much harm, and reverse the trend in the future. As Paul says in Philippians 3:13 'but one thing I do, forgetting what lies behind and press on to what lies ahead'.

My first exposure to the streams of God's healing grace was at Tipton Street Methodist Church. Healing came through the acceptance I received in the relationships I formed there. It was then that I accepted the new life and salvation that Jesus offers. And then a little later on, the ministry of Reverend Selwyn Hughes and Wholeness Through Christ, each one being a stream of God's grace and love that brought healing and hope to me.

In fact my Christian journey is best described as a journey of healing. Even the process of writing this book has itself been a voyage of discovering greater self-awareness, which has helped me to reflect and pray about painful areas of my life that have not yet been healed. In a typical act of hubris, before I started writing this, I really thought I was over some of these areas. Perhaps that wasn't so true.

So, my early Christian experience and this book are a small selection of the many streams of healing I've been exposed to, particularly but not exclusively, during my meltdowns in York.

Some have been Christian, some secular.
Perhaps one of the most powerful streams was given to me while I was on retreat at St Antony's Priory in Durham. The passage is 1 Kings 19. The story is of God's healing streams in the desert when Elijah was suffering with depression. I frequently use this passage as a vehicle for prayer using my imagination as I walk with Elijah through the story.
I have found imaginative prayer to be a healing stream. You simply find a safe place, sit down and imagine yourself in a particular Bible story. Using your senses to imagine how things might have looked, felt, smelt, sounded and tasted.
The story actually begins in chapter 18 with Elijah proving the power of the Lord over Baal. Elijah was the principal prophet of the Lord (Yahweh) during the reign of King Ahab. Ahab had been influenced by his wife Jezebel whom he allowed to build a temple dedicated to Baal in Samaria, complete with pagan altar (1 Kings 16:32). Jezebel and Ahab later instigated open opposition to the Lord. Altars were torn down, true prophets of the lord were killed and Elijah fled for his life.
That great prophet, Elijah, had an amazing, pioneering ministry; standing up to the false prophets of Baal and the wicked Queen Jezebel. He showed the power of God at the altar on Mount Carmel defeating Baal and making the false prophets look ridiculous, yet all the same, he found himself running in peril, running from the conflict he'd become embroiled in, running headlong into the desert for safety. The story as it unfolds resonates powerfully with mine, because, just like Elijah, I wanted to run away and find sanctuary from all I was going through.
We pick up the story in 1 Kings 19: 4-5:

'He himself went on a day's journey into the desert. He came to a broom tree, sat down under it and prayed that he might die. 'I have

had enough Lord,' he said. 'Take my life; I am no better than my ancestors.' Then he lay down under the tree and fell asleep.'

Through prayer, I was in Elijah's story. He had run away and was now in the desert. As I now engaged with the story, healing streams of love were to fall on me. Elijah wanted to die, he had had enough. I too had had enough of the challenge, the conflict and the criticism. Elijah had fallen asleep beneath a broom bush. I too spent much of my time sleeping. I was so washed out. I'd go to bed at night and sleep solidly. Then I would get up, go downstairs and sleep on the sofa. And yet the tiredness would not leave me. This went on for weeks and weeks and weeks; my life becoming one long period of sleep. I was in a complete state of meltdown.

All at once an angel touched him and said, "Get up and eat." He looked around, and there by his head was a cake of bread baked over hot coals, and a jar of water. He ate and drank and then lay down again. The angel of the Lord came back a second time and touched him and said, "Get up and eat, for the journey is too much for you." So he got up and ate and drank. 1 Kings 19: 5-8

I was sustained by people whom I describe as angels; by my wife Alison, by my family and friends. People sent flowers and cards. One lady on the way into town brought cakes round. People also looked after Alison while I was ill. All of this I appreciated greatly. Pastoral care is a powerful healing stream.
But Elijah's angel had emphasised that the journey was too hard for him. And that was it. This journey was too hard for me. I just couldn't do it anymore. I was depressed, exhausted and burnt out with nowhere to go.
Strengthened by that food, he travelled for forty days and forty nights until he reached Horeb [Sinai] the mountain of God.

There he went into a cave and spent the night. 1 Kings 19: 8-9 After sleeping and eating under the bush, Elijah journeyed for forty days and nights to Mt Sinai, where the law had been given to Moses. It's no coincidence that the children of Israel had also spent forty years' wandering in the desert. I too was in that wilderness, in that land between two places. I was in a state of meltdown like so many before me: Elijah's forty days, and the Israelites' forty years. I couldn't go forward and I couldn't go back. My mind would turn around in circles for days on end without going anywhere.

It was in Elijah's cave that I started to find hope for healing and renewal. It was the whisper of God. It occurred to me that this cave of Elijah's was a cave of contemplation and it was the possibility of this whisper of God in contemplative prayer that started to stir my spirit.

'The Lord said, "Go out and stand on the mountain in the presence of the Lord, for the Lord is about to pass by." Then a great and powerful wind tore the mountains apart and shattered the rocks before the Lord, but the Lord was not in the wind. After the wind there was an earthquake, but the Lord was not in the earthquake. After the earthquake came a fire, but the Lord was not in the fire. And after the fire came a gentle whisper.' 1 Kings 19: 11-12

At that time my safe place was St Bede's. My spiritual director was also part of the team at there. I was encouraged to enrol on a course called Personal and Spiritual development (PSD), a two year course, one night a week during term time. The point of it is to develop Christian people personally and spiritually. Two sides of the same coin.

As I descended into the dryness, the bleakness and also the mystery of depression, PSD on a Thursday evening was the only thing that I could do. It was the thing that sustained me on that long journey. I used to force myself to go. There was one session that became too much, but that was when they were all dancing, which I dislike at the best of times. I had to leave the room; in fact I staggered to the toilets and was physically sick. That was the only night I had such a reaction and they really looked after me. I found it a really safe place to be me. In terms of contemplative prayer and the desire and the deepening of faith this course was amazing. I found those Thursday evenings to be a healing stream. I found the still, small voice of God to be so powerful and so wonderful. As I regained mental and physical strength I started to think more deeply about Elijah's journey back from the cave. In the story he leaves the desert, but comes back via a different route. He'd had his wilderness experience, encountered the whisper of God and now he was coming back via a different route through the desert.

Coming back a different way…

I did recover enough to return to work as I felt I could enjoy a more balanced work life experience. I also believed I could handle the pressures of pioneering ministry. (In total I had been off work for six months and I had returned to work for almost a year.)

But it wasn't long before I felt my energy levels begin to drop and once again I was melting down and beginning to experience the darkness of depression. I was very confused and wondered why. I was indeed returning through the dryness of the desert. This journey seemed to be taking me towards early retirement due to my health.

At the end of Elijah's journey we read how much his ministry had changed from the pioneer who had taken on the forces of opposition, conflict and criticism, to Elijah the enabler who put his mantle around Elisha, encouraging him in his ministry. I was so struck by that. Elijah had been on this transformative journey: from pioneer, to burnt out, to coming back as an enabler. It was a journey that mirrored my own so exactly. I was aware that I could engage with people, encourage and motivate them. I could help build community and put teams of people together. I could do all of these things. But the added dimension now was a greater self-awareness, an interest in mindfulness, and an interest in contemplative prayer. I was coming back a different way with a renewed and reinvigorated walk with God. Ready to retire - a new chapter in my life and ministry. The only way I can describe the experience was being born again.

Again.

I'd found that depression is a devastating, slippery illness to have. I'd experienced my second bout of depression in York differently to the other episodes. It felt I was living in a desert or a really dark tunnel. It was like being in one of those long old canal tunnels where you can't see anything apart from a tiny speck of light at the end. Gradually that little bit of light was getting brighter and brighter and brighter until I stood at the mouth of the dark tunnel. I looked behind and saw darkness and nothing good at all. I looked forward and saw something beautiful, something bright, something exciting. I saw countryside and I heard birds singing. It was like there was a way forward stretching ahead of me but occasionally, just around the corner there was a lock gate. Periodically I'd sink and have another dark day, another dark night of the soul. But the lock gate would help me to move up and then go forward again. It's true to say that my journey has been a series of lock gates, of renewal and healing and perhaps most importantly of understanding some of the dynamics of that healing as well.

During my journey I was blessed with a sympathetic and understanding doctor. If only more doctors were as sensitive to the pressures from work and society on people, and were so motivated to help their patients. As a result of my GP's intervention, I was introduced to mindfulness and Cognitive Behavioural Therapy.

The term cognitive encompasses thought processes as well as knowledge or perception. Cognitive therapists emphasise examination of the thoughts and beliefs connected to our moods, behaviours, physical experiences, and to the events in our lives. A central idea in cognitive therapy is that our perception of an event or experience powerfully affects our emotional, behavioural and physiological responses to it. For me this understanding of CBT resonates with Paul's words in Romans 12:2 'Do not be conformed to the things of this world but be transformed by the renewal of your minds'.

CBT allows a person to talk through their problems. As part of the work, the overlap between thoughts, feelings and behaviours is broken down. Once you've identified the trigger for negative feelings and thoughts, you are in a position to adapt and change. You probably can't change all the patterning of low self-esteem, but you can learn to spot the signs and avoid spiralling down into a vicious cycle of self-recrimination and reproach. I think what I liked about CBT was that it had a clear methodology to explore personal issues. I learned a lot about myself: that my early years weren't the best; that a sound foundation hadn't been laid down, that I'd found my identity in working, achieving and in being successful. I'd achieved great things both in industry and in ministry. Ministry is a caring profession, and I soaked it all up like a sponge, listening to people, having a good pastoral heart and a good pastoral ministry. Equally, I see myself as a pioneer, I always have done, looking at new ways of working, and enabling the church to be a healing community, making it relevant to those who are not yet Christians.

During my period of recovery, both my therapist and doctor

recommended a book on mindfulness meditation. Mindfulness was also discussed on PSD at St Bede's. Mindfulness is a discipline that guides you into the present moment, the goal is to calm the soul and open oneself to prayerful activity. It is another means of avoiding distraction and the intrusive, negative thoughts that blight the lives of people like me who suffer from burnout and depression.

Another important aspect to my recovery was provided to me by the London Institute of Contemporary Christianity. A gentleman named Paul Vellor mentored me through some difficult times. He has been really helpful in thinking about how to move forward at the most troubling moments. Paul was generous with his time and incredibly helpful in guiding my way forward. He encouraged me to think about forgiveness. I realised then that forgiveness is an ongoing process.

Of course, I can't talk about healing without talking about my friends and family. Alison has been a rock throughout our marriage, but went above and beyond the call of duty when I was burnt out. She kept everything going and supported me no matter what I said or did. I couldn't have done any of this without her, and I love her now more than I ever did. The rest of my family have also been supportive and generous. They've helped, they've hosted and they've reached out to both of us when times have been difficult. Most of all, what my family and friends have allowed is space to rest, like Elijah under the bush. They gave me time to recover my health and my energy, and knew instinctively how close was too close, and how far was too far.

But perhaps most important of all has been the course in Personal and Spiritual Development I have been taking at St Bede's. While Paul Golightly at St Anthony's Priory helped signpost my way back using scripture, St Bede's offered the vehicle with which to do it. I've given a brief outline of the elements of the course and the way they have led me into a deeper life in prayer and a more contemplative outlook on life. It's been really helpful to think my way through biblical and personal issues, but it has also been part of a process of becoming more reflective. As I went through these modules, I learned so much more about myself and the role prayer could play in my life and the life of others.

WAYS OF PRAYING: This module introduced various ways of praying and looked at the whole process of prayer and how it fits into our lives.

DEEPENING OUR PRAYER: We moved on to ways we could deepen our prayer. We also looked at some of the difficulties that can occur in prayer and how we can work creatively with them.

IMAGES OF GOD AND SELF: We all carry around inside us images of God; some are creative and life-enhancing whilst others are less helpful. They largely determine how we see and relate to ourselves, to others and to our world. In this module we explored and unpacked our images of God, seeing how they shape, and are shaped by our life experiences.

DISCERNMENT: Drawing on the life and tradition of St Ignatius and using his rules of discernment, we sought to grow in awareness of God's movement in our daily lives.

DECISION MAKING: Building on the previous module on discernment we explored the process of decision making in faith, in the hope that we may become freer to respond to God in our life choices.

TAKING IT FURTHER, TAKING IT DEEPER: We ended the course with an opportunity to engage in a 'Retreat In Daily Life'. The aim was to help us discover how to use the learning from the last 2 years for ourselves and for others in daily life.

I think, with all this help, with all these different streams of healing, I'm getting better (or at least a little more resilient). Being a sensitive person, conflict and criticism are tricky things to cope with at the best of times and I think that would be true for most ministers and people in caring professions. Because we're sensitive, we are vulnerable to criticism and conflict. I've found it is a matter of detaching myself from the situation, disengaging from it and sometimes walking away; whenever that's possible, politely, without making the conflict worse. So I think I've resolved that in my mind. I don't have to take it personally because really, it's that person's history and hard wiring which is causing them to react in a particular way. Their issues and their journey make them the people they are today. I can't be responsible for their reactions; I can only own my own, and that's one of the things I've learnt as time has gone on. This is where the word of God cuts right through, 'love others as you love yourself'. I always skipped over this too quickly. I've now learned that you do need to have a healthy self-respect, a healthy self-regard and healthy ways of looking forward in order to function and in order to live with other people. I can now step back. I don't have to engage with this conflict. It's not my responsibility to own what you're throwing at me now. It's about engaging with issues not personalities. It's about knowing your responsibilities and not allowing others to undermine them. It's about identifying and nurturing people to enable them to flourish.
As my healing journey gathered pace, I started to think about a new way of expressing my mission. I've hinted at it many times

through this book. The fruit of all my pain and hurt, but also of the love of God, of family and friends, of the care shown me by the London Institute of Contemporary Christianity, St Bede's and St Anthony's; by my doctor, therapist, my personal trainer, Victoria Allington at the gym and the warmth of the Christian people at York Community Church. The York Community Church has been a real blessing to Alison and me through their style in leadership, Bible teaching and worship, they are a very healing community who gave me permission to be myself with no judgement or expectation.

Moving into retirement is a landmark in a person's life. The Methodist Church is good at celebrating rites of passage. On this occasion it was two-fold. First of all The York churches arranged a celebration service at Lidgett Grove Methodist Church. It was a wonderful occasion with a full church, lively worship and good preaching from my dear friend the Reverend Graham Carter.

The second was a few weeks later at Copmanthorpe Methodist Church during the harvest festival celebrations. The church wanted to acknowledge our moving into the village, affirm my ministry and acknowledge my retirement. They had commissioned a very good friend of mine Mrs Jill Solwich, who is a member at Copmanthorpe Methodist and a local artist, to create a work of art to celebrate the journey that the Lord was about to take me on

Both services were very different but together they acknowledged my past ministry and celebrated what was to come.

I can now rest and heal. With the help of a very special family we have been able to buy a lovely bungalow in Copmanthorpe. Good friends have helped us to decorate it throughout and my late father gave us most of the money to renovate it. Quite simply, it is a miracle.

Chapter Nine
Imagine Projects

"So we rebuilt the wall till all of it reached half its height, for the people worked with all their heart." Nehemiah 4:6

It seemed to me that just as Elijah handed over his mantle to Elisha, perhaps I could find a means of passing to others some of the things I'd learned. When I read the story of Nehemiah coming back from Babylon to restore the walls around Jerusalem, it spoke to me so much. I have preached on this book many times, leading congregations through a theological reflection on project management as found in Nehemiah. I love this book of the Bible. Every time I read it, it speaks to me.

I was thinking deeply about all of these things. In the context of being a deacon, I realised what I loved most of all was bringing the love of God to people outside of the walls of the church through projects. This was the genesis of Imagine Projects. It originated in my dark night of the soul and in my recovery and the support I had received. Imagine Projects is, in itself, a healing stream.

I'm a professional project manager and an ordained minister. I've had years of experience in industry carrying out a variety of projects. I've also had experience as a minister with community-based projects, right back to when I was a lay worker after I'd left Cliff College. It seemed to me that I had a wealth of knowledge, training, experience and resources to share. From the suffering I have gone through and the desire to share these experiences as a means to serve, Imagine Projects was born. The conception of Imagine Projects is the conclusion of many decades of experience, reading, training, thought and prayer. I offer it as a method of delivering meaningful provision for individuals and communities.

I've always been a big picture person, so it's like seeing a big vision, but also being able to see the pathways to get there. The name 'Imagine' came to me while sitting with my lap top in the bar at the Marriott Hotel in York. I found the hotel a nice place to go for a coffee and it was there while reading Nehemiah that I was once again drawn to the big picture he'd had in his mind for rebuilding the walls around Jerusalem. I kept saying to myself, 'Imagine if this, imagine if that.' I was just looking for a phrase that captured what I believed could happen, whether it's a church, charity or any other organisation. An organisation or individual has to dream a dream, imagine what could be. Vision starts with an organisation or individual becoming aware that something isn't working and imagining how much better it could be. It begins with where you are now. It's going on that journey and taking other people along with you. The foundation of Imagine Projects was right there in Nehemiah – rebuilding something through team work and a sound project that seemed to be in ruins.

As I have mentioned, one of the things that has come out of my CBT therapy is a growing self awareness. In the past, whenever I achieved something I would instantly put a lid on it and move on to the next thing without really taking stock, reflecting on it and appreciating it. As soon as one project was finished, I'd be straight off on to the next one. I've had some very good achievements over the years, and having the confidence to put Imagine together came out of those accomplishments. I suppose it forced me to reflect on the positives. It comes back to sober reflection which leads to learning to love yourself so that you might love others.

On one level Imagine Projects is a record of my experience, a tangible testimony. I've managed many projects in a variety of contexts, in business and the charity sector so I feel I'm in a position to offer some good consultancy to others. There's also very much a creative element of gathering all the milestones of my journey and building something new from them.

As a Methodist Diaconal Minister (Deacon), although retired from the 'active work' and in my role as a project manager, I've come to believe that servant leadership is the foundation on which all good leadership is based, developed and exercised. A relational and collaborative service model.

In recent years much has been said and written about service in the public, private and charity sectors. Popular teaching and thinking on leadership seems to have an emphasis on a relational model. As Christians, we turn to Jesus as our role model for servant leadership. The principle focus of His leadership was to point away from Himself and toward others. This is the perfect model to adopt, as it points beyond ourselves and is directed towards and inspired by others. Truly serving others requires putting ourselves and our desires aside whilst looking for ways and opportunities to do what is best for others. Having said that, self-flourishing is really important, because to help others flourish, servant leaders should put measures in place to flourish themselves. We see Nehemiah do this as he prays, delegates and equips others so that he and his project are protected especially during periods of conflict. There is a balance to be found. It would not be helpful to fall into the trap of insisting on 'looking after number one' or asking 'what is in it for me?' or in working oneself into the ground. Rather, service begins with prayer and appropriate and healthy self respect.

In Matthew 22:39 we read, 'love your neighbour as yourself.' A servant leader needs to look for ways and opportunities to do what is best for other people, whilst having a healthy awareness of their own needs, qualities, strengths and weaknesses. In my experience relational, serving leaders produce relational, serving leaders. There has to be inheritance and growth just as we see in Elisha's double portion of Elijah's spirit in 2 Kings 2:9. The request by Elisha for a double portion of Elijah's spirit refers to Elisha being doubly blessed in his life and ministry. Interestingly scripture records exactly twice as many miracles carried out through Elisha (28) than through Elijah (14). When organisations build people in this fashion, those people actively seek to serve others around them. This is critical to the ultimate growth and success of any organisation.

The Imagine model of servant leadership encourages, educates and enables organisations and people to engage and flourish. Imagine teaches and trains people to be the best they can be. It imagines what would happen if people were gripped with joy and gratitude by the difference a programme of projects could make to companies, charities and communities and the people they serve. It imagines what would happen if you created a community where people felt safe to be who they are and encouraged to become all they can be. It imagines what would happen if you discovered untapped resources in your community and used them to be good news to the people in it. It imagines the future.

Imagine is an accessible and flexible framework to work from. It uses an acronym for the word 'Imagine' to create a project life cycle:

I = Inception
M = Map
A = Action
G = Governing

I = Identity
N = Nurture
E = End

Each word in the acronym represents a stage of the project life cycle.

A key aspect to the Imagine process is to identify and nurture talent. It's about keeping good people on board during the project. One of the things I love is to see people flourish. Giving someone a part in a project enables them to grow. I want to go out and ask people, 'How do you want to be involved in this? Would you like to do a bit of marketing? Would you like to do a bit of admin? Would you like to make some bacon sarnies? Would you like to interview somebody in the street? There are so many opportunities for people to flourish, really, and for them to take risks and say, 'OK, from a volunteering point of view, I can do this, and it doesn't matter, same as if it were a paid job.' So if you do get someone to take a risk and say, 'OK, I'll take a risk on going to church.' They take their risk by coming along.

This brings in a whole host of other stories. Issues about welcome and hospitality and the organisation's values. Welcoming, accepting and valuing people for who they are. So that's where I try to work. Encouraging people to take risks, to have a go, realising it doesn't matter if you mess up. If you get along, you get along, if you don't like it, you don't like it. In my projects, older and younger people have been involved. It depends what interests them, a cafe or community cinema for instance. They're happy because firstly it makes a difference to their community, and secondly it's something that they enjoy. For instance, we worked with one woman who had confidence issues. We put her through the food safety course, got her qualified and now she has seen what she can do. From the confidence she's gained, she wants to apply for a couple of jobs. As you can imagine, that is so satisfying for us and potentially life changing for her. It's interesting that all of my projects are about empowering people; it's all about giving hope and the right tools to people. We can enable people to grow. We can form a community which meets real needs and answers direct questions. We start the journey in the heart of the community. We put together a strategic plan, and that in turn kick starts all the other projects. That's the exciting bit. You do the community survey because you really want to know the answers. When you bother to ask someone's views, someone who would normally get overlooked, it makes such a massive difference.

I can't claim the community survey as an original idea, but I am passionate about it. I think to understand what you have to do, you need to identify where people are hurting and where the needs are. You need to see where the gaps in provision are so that you can start to fill them without replication. So the survey helps an organisation to get more deeply involved with their community. The survey takes an organisation into a more missionary mode. It enables them to speak to wider groups. It helps them get a much deeper understanding to see what's going badly and what can be done to improve things.

Time and time again, the surveys identify loneliness as being incredibly prevalent. From a personal perspective, this is really important to me, I've lived with loneliness for a large part of my life, especially when I was growing up. You can be lonely in a crowd, so it's not always about going to things; it's much more internal. It's about how you feel about yourself as much as anything. It's more about a mismatch of relationships both in respect of yourself and other people.

How do you engage with people over the long term, so that they can feel good about themselves? I have discovered that there is more to addressing loneliness than providing coffee mornings (important though they are). You could provide a coffee morning, but people who are lonely, who are feeling scared, frightened or vulnerable are not going to go. So part of the Imagine way is to say, 'How do you imagine meeting that hard-to-reach person? What could you do if they wanted some help?' The community survey might highlight some unexpected answers.

When forming the questionnaire it is important to visit different groups. The doctor might say, for example, 'put a question in about drug abuse, lack of exercise or loneliness and social isolation.' In parallel with that there's a lack of places in the area where people can meet. Perhaps debt is an issue, or employment opportunities. Part of the resulting research should focus on that wider picture and to try and dovetail it with the narrower view, so that the strands come together. Then you can work out what you can realistically achieve. For instance, there wouldn't be much use having an all-singing, all-dancing youth club if the volunteers are all in their sixties. People must be at the heart of it, you have to think about what resources are available and what's realistic in that context. Part of the survey is coming back and saying, 'There's five or six things here, what is achievable for us? The key objective in this example is to help alleviate loneliness. Then you ask, 'What would be the other things out of the research that you could do?' That starts the whole process again, really.

But Imagine can be anybody's journey. On a personal level, imagine a one-to-one interview in which the following questions are asked:

- Imagine what you would like to be?
- Imagine what you would like to do?
- What don't you like about now?

That's where journeys begin; identifying what you don't like about now and what the steps could be to get you to the next stage. So Imagine can be a therapeutic pathway for people. In terms of outcomes, perhaps it's whether you need some qualifications or to change your job and so on. It's asking where you are now, and what is your vision for a good outcome. So how you put that conception into a project lifecycle can be very personal. How do you identify and nurture what you really are? What's the action plan? How do you monitor it to check that you're on the right track? It is deeply personal as well as corporate.

From a theological perspective it's incarnation. God came down to earth in the person of Jesus; Christ works with us in this world, and hopefully we can engage with Him. We can ask, 'Where are the injustices?' I'd say loneliness is an injustice. People shouldn't be lonely because we're made to be in relationships, with God first and foremost, but also with ourselves and with each other. With prayer and a loving heart and if motivated to help everyone come into a right relationship with God, we transform lives and bring people out of the misery of loneliness into a promised land of loving relationships. That's one of the aspects that I hope will come out of Imagine Projects.

This isn't some grandiose scheme for reforming the world. It's simply one step at a time. Creating Imagine from a pile of ruins is an achievement. That's my reflection. The old me wouldn't have done that. I mean straight up, this is a really rounded piece of work. It's a question of taking that forward now and integrating the concepts, building people up and getting them into the right relationships with God, with themselves and with one another.

Chapter Ten

Hills of Difficulty, Springs of Refreshment

"This hill, though high, I covet to ascend;
The difficulty will not me offend.
For I perceive the way to life lies here.
Come, pluck up, heart; let's neither faint nor fear.
Better, though difficult, the right way to go,
Than wrong, though easy, where the end is woe."
John Bunyan, Pilgrim's Progress

In John Bunyan's classic allegory, The Pilgrim's Progress, Christian comes to the Hill of Difficulty after he is released from his burden at the Cross. Bunyan reminds us to walk in the light of revealed truth and take the next challenge God puts before us, no matter how intimidating.

The Hill of Difficulty represents the tough consequences of pursuing a dream, obeying the truth, and following Jesus. If we're walking with Jesus, at some stage we will encounter the hill. On my journey I have discovered the hard way that success is not about attaining perfection because God loves us and asks us to be faithful not "successful". Success therefore is a positive response to the next challenge. Success involves a series of steps; ongoing acts of obedience, faithfulness, and growth.

It seems that the message we all hear so often is we should avoid struggle, pain and suffering and that a life in which you experience these things is severely short-changing you. This is in direct opposition to what the Bible says. The Hill of Difficulty tests and strengthens our faith and proves the reality of the spiritual resources we have in Christ. In Bunyan's words:
"The hill, though high, I covet to ascend, The difficulty will not me offend; For I perceive the way of life lies here. Come, pluck up heart, let's neither faint nor fear; Better, though difficult, the right way to go, Than wrong, though easy, where the end is woe."
On Christian's journey difficulty arises. Formalist and Hypocrisy are quite willing to accompany Christian as long as the journey does not present any obstacles. In the shadow of the Hill of Difficulty however, they are both unwilling to continue with Christian. Bunyan notes that at the bottom of the hill is a spring. Both the hill and the spring come from the hand of God. Our loving Father providentially places difficulties and trials in our path, desiring that we rise to them and don't try to avoid them. As Paul states in 2 Timothy 4:7, we have a race to run, a fight to fight and a faith to grab firm hold of. In God's mercy and goodness he provides all we need for this race, this fight, this faith. He gives us all we need to make it up and over our hills.
Before Christian begins climbing, he takes refreshment at the spring. This picture comes from the prophet Isaiah, who speaks of a refreshing spring as he describes God's care of His people in the midst of affliction:

"They shall neither hunger nor thirst,
Neither heat nor sun shall strike them;
For He who has mercy on them will lead them,
Even by the springs of water He will guide them."
Isaiah 49:10

The Spring is a testimony to the goodness of God in all He brings us through. No matter how steep or high our own difficulties may seem, we can trust that God will work through it all to our good and sanctification.

This book has explored my hills of difficulty through the lens of my own journey and spiritual development. I've explored the hills and the springs that God has placed along the way and the lessons I've learned about myself and my Lord.

I have been a Methodist for over thirty years and hold dear in my heart the core doctrines of the Methodist Church as expressed in the 'Four All's' of Methodism below, and in the 'Deed of Union'[8].

The 'Four All's' of Methodism
- All need to be saved
- All can be saved
- All can know they are saved
- All can be saved to the uttermost

If God can take the life of a broken lad from the Black Country, he can change the life of anyone. The good news is 'All Can Be' and that has been my motivation for all the projects I've been privileged to serve through and for those I have yet to carry out. For with the Lord the best is always yet to come.

For example, when I was a senior manager working in tool hire in Nottingham I remember visiting one of my customers. David was a buyer for a medium-sized construction company. We had met on numerous occasions and it was his turn to buy lunch. I used to wonder if there was such a thing as a free lunch in the world of business? Call me cynical but I presume there

---

[8] See Appendix 5

is always the hidden agenda of gaining more business. Nothing wrong with that at all. On this occasion, I could tell David was distracted so I plucked up the courage to ask him what was on his mind. I found myself being harangued as he told me in no uncertain terms how vicious, fickle and hideous he considered God to be. He had some fairly cogent points to make and he made them with real vim and vigour. There was no doubt about it: God was either a complete phoney or a total monster, and to believe in him was either an act of vanity or madness.

Much to David's surprise, I could only agree with him. In fact I went further and suggested we had another cup of coffee to toast the demise of this ugly, vain god in whom I also disbelieved with equal vigour. Dave sat there, stunned.

I said that I would be privileged to tell him about the God of Jesus Christ in whom I do believe and who has been my saviour on numerous occasions. This was the God who did not send the trials and sufferings which so many people experience. On the contrary, I have experienced a God who is not disinterested, immune or unaffected by the pain and tragedy we all experience. This was a God who was not just concerned with whether we were good or bad, peevishly keeping some sort of heavenly log book and endlessly checking on our behaviour, only happy if we were forever abasing ourselves before him and asking for forgiveness and mercy, but a God who loved the world so much that he came in human vulnerability to save it, not condemn it. A God who was involved in the joys and sorrows of human lives; a God, in fact, who knew what it was like to be human. A God who reached down to earth so that we could reach up to heaven; a God who made everything, and then graciously offered himself that we might all share everything with Him. This is a God who keeps no record of our wrongs.

David did not become a Christian there and then. He didn't run out of the café singing "Praise the Lord" but he was both surprised and delighted, cheered and challenged, by a different way of looking at God – that is through the lens of Jesus. For me Jesus is best understood as God's way of getting to know God.

I've spoken a lot about my journey of faith. I now want to take a moment to speak about my Saviour – Jesus of Nazareth. Since the day of my conversion at Tipton Street, Jesus has been my friend and my saviour. When I talk about God I am talking about God as He is revealed in Jesus. God became a human being – Jesus. In Jesus God lived, died and rose again to offer new life and healing of all the wounds that we carry. Jesus identifies with us because He shared our human experience. He is completely God and completely human. In the person of Jesus, heaven and earth meet together. He is not simply a public speaker, a miracle worker, a prophet or even superman, He is God come down to earth. Technically referred to as the incarnation.

I am aware that, like David, many people have never encountered God in this way. As a result it's easy to see why the whole idea of God doesn't seem to fit into the mess that is life for most of us. How great it is that God shares our human suffering and joy! Because He became a human being like us; it changes things. It does not make our suffering any less painful, but it does prevent us from supposing God is separate, to blame or immune from it all.

It also tells us about God's longing. How else could God communicate His desire to enjoy a relationship with us, except by coming among us?

God comes to us in Jesus to bring a new way of understanding and appreciating life. The life we have may be good and beautiful, the challenge of the Christian faith is that only God can satisfy our deeper longings. Many people like me have experienced a deep frustration inside because they have become far too busy, too frantic, too driven and have within them a cry for healing, joy and peace. I have discovered that only God can properly be the centre of life. This may feel uncomfortable because even though many people recoil from Jesus, reject him and ridicule Him, this truth resonates with that aching hunger; a hunger that so many try to quell with addictive behaviour, including work and endless activity. I did exactly this and became ill as a result.

When I discovered the love and acceptance that can be found in God, I also discovered a deep assurance that no matter what happens in this life, especially in the darkest moments of depression, burnout, doubt and despair, I was loved unconditionally. We are all unconditionally loved by God.

This is the great message of the Christian faith: that God loves us all and nothing can separate us from His love. We don't need to earn it. There is nothing we can do to stop it. There is nothing we need to do to receive it, just accept it as a free gift. Salvation is complete, unearned and offers the adventure of growth and discipleship.

Even if all this seems too good to be true and you can't accept it, or even understand it and choose to reject it, it is always there waiting for you. You are loved just the same.

We will never be forced into acknowledging God in the way I have described. It should never be a hard sell. However, the offer has to be made. And whether we accept it or not, God goes on loving us.

The greatest sign of this staggering truth is the death of Jesus on the cross. In an age when so many people know so little about the Christian faith, most people are still aware of this: that at the end of His life Jesus submitted to the most painful and cruel death. It is the ultimate sign of God's involvement with human beings. God shares everything. God receives the worst rejection of all. Jesus comes to us with arms outstretched ready to embrace, and offering words of comfort and forgiveness to all who are prepared to listen. This is the God we find in Jesus: pure love.

The message that Jesus pours out on the cross with His own shed blood is that we are loved, accepted and forgiven. We are loved even when we don't feel lovable, or have never felt loved before, or don't even know what love feels like.

We are all accepted regardless of our race, gender, sexuality, caste, class or creed. We are all forgiven for all the things that have wounded and obscured God's image within us.

I have discovered that forgiveness is a very powerful healing stream that refreshes one's life. Forgiveness is never easy but it is necessary in order to live a whole life.

This is what David and I chatted about over a coffee. Forgiveness and a positive way of looking at God; an accessible way, a way that is both old and new. Old, because it is the Christian story that has been told for two thousand years. New, because each of us needs to hear it for ourselves in a way that we can relate to.

A key question is this: will you receive this gift? We must be able to choose whether to accept it or not, because to have a gift forced upon you is not love at all. We have a choice because we have freedom and if we are not sure, or it has never been communicated clearly or even if we hear but choose to reject it, the door is still open. The welcome mat is still out on the porch, the table laid, your place prepared. The ticket to the party is always valid: we simply have to say yes and we are welcomed warmly into the arms of Jesus.

From my experience and my understanding of the Bible people don't seem to need systems, rituals and programs to discover God and to be ok with God. They don't need to search for his love - although there is much evidence to support the fact that plenty of people are searching for healing, love, meaning and purpose to their lives. Neither is discovering God solely for those who don't already believe. I am always discovering God in new and deeper ways. The discovery of God is something we should not stop aiming for. I know that God is never finished with us, we are constantly journeying. I may not know what lies ahead of me, what I might face or what I will learn but I will put my hand in God's and walk towards a deeper relationship with Him.

When we talk about knowing God, we need look no further than Jesus, the one through whom everything was made. He came to us a human being so that normal people like you and I can know God's character and grow in personal relationship with Him.

This is the Christian claim that is the heartbeat of the universe: all the purposes of God as revealed in the life, death and resurrection of Jesus are best understood as a declaration of love, delivered personally to each one of us. It is an invitation to live a new and abundant life. Either this is true, or we are deluded and the whole Christian edifice comes tumbling down. But because it is true it is the foundation, the centre upon which everything in our lives should be built. Everything changes. Contrary to all the sensible advice of an anxious, competitive and increasingly lonely world, there is such a thing as a free lunch. God himself has laid the table, everyone is invited and all things are ready. It is so simple. It is a choice to accept or decline your personal invitation. The question is, "will you accept the invitation?"

Appendix 1a

Bilton Grange Project - The old

Bilton Grange – the old building prior to demolition

Appendix 1b

Bilton Grange Project - The new

The Acorns – the new building on completion

Appendix 3b

Discovery Family Centre Design

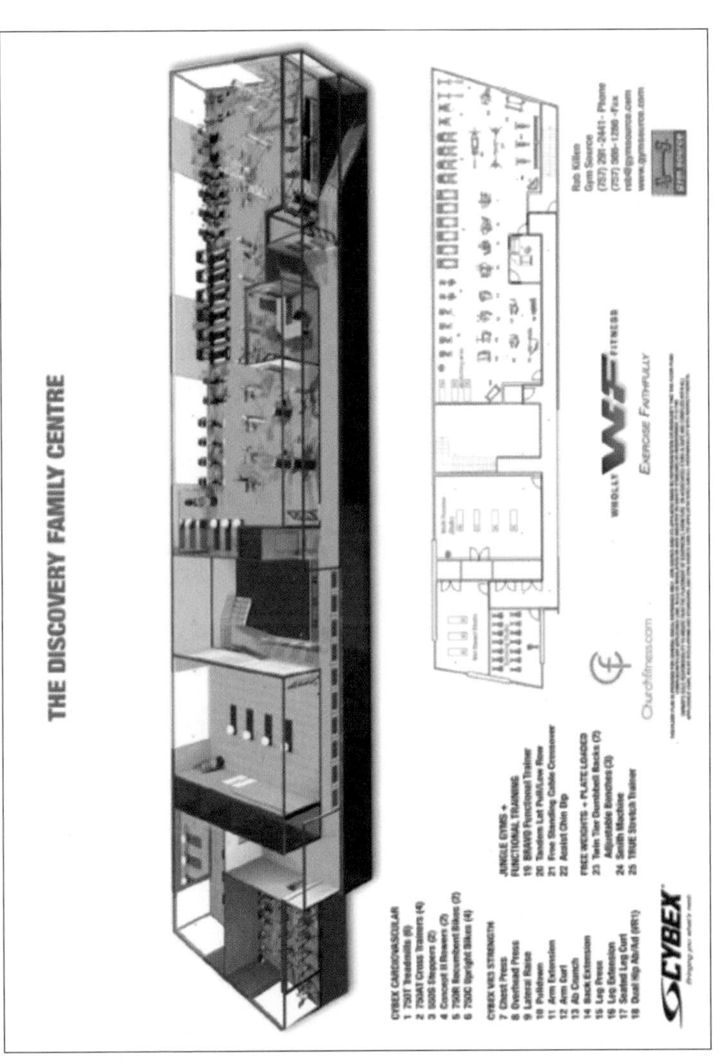

The design for the proposed health and fitness suite in the Discovery Family Centre

Appendix 4
New Monasticism and Fresh Expressions of Church

Tuesday, 22 November, 2011
(From the Fresh Expressions Web Site)
Rev. Graham Cray

Today's changing culture calls for a huge diversity and range of fresh expressions of church. Graham Cray explores one particular flavour of fresh expression in an article from the Reader Magazine, November 2011.
Anglican priests and parishes have the 'cure of souls' of the whole parish, not just of those who go to church. So we at Fresh Expressions are challenging the churches to ask a key question. Who is not being touched or reached by the existing ministry of the local churches, whether that be through a neighbourhood ministry or through engaging with networks of common interest? As churches begin to engage with this question, they hopefully develop a discipline of local prayerful listening as they explore the possibility of establishing a fresh expression – a new congregation or church plant.
The whole point of a fresh expression is that it is appropriate to its context and is particularly for those not being effectively engaged by the churches already. Models that are being used elsewhere may be appropriate, but the most important thing is to work out what is appropriate for where you are. We have to be open to diversity and to imagining new things. You can't simply 'launch' a fresh expression somewhere without any thought as to whether it's the right shape for the context and culture it finds itself in.
A number of things are needed when looking to establish a fresh expression of church and that's where the history of monastic movements can help us. Firstly, we are seeking to establish a

community rather than an event. Church is a community of which we are a part, not an event we go to. Biblically of course Christians don't so much go to church as they are Church. Sometimes they are Church gathered together and sometimes they are solitary, scattered as they go about their daily lives, but the Church is the primary community to which they belong. Sadly some people do attend local churches as no more than a regular event in their calendar but, properly understood, a church is a community to help people become lifelong disciples of Jesus, which is far more than attending services or staking their initial claim to faith.

We then have to consider how – in our sophisticated and in some ways novel culture– we form the habits of a way of life that will shape us as followers of Jesus? The evangelical tradition, among others, has put a huge emphasis on personal disciplines of daily prayer and Bible reading. These are vital, but to sustain them today I believe we also need something corporate; regular contexts of mutual encouragement, support and challenge. In our very individualistic society we need community if we are to sustain discipleship in our daily lives. The expression 'one another' appears frequently in the New Testament, 34 times in Paul's letters alone. What a number of us are thinking is that every church member who is serious about being a follower of Jesus might be part of a small, mutually accountable group, where they are real with one another about the areas of their lives where discipleship is hard, and positive in encouraging and praying for each other. What we might particularly learn from the monastic movement is some appropriate rule or rhythm of life.

It is obedience to the Holy Spirit from day to day that grows the fruits of the Spirit, and the local church is the community which supports and fosters that growth. The primary purpose of these small communities within a local church is to seek to live in daily obedience to Jesus. A group of Christian disciples know they face certain pressures at work, home and in different areas of their lives. By covenanting to meet regularly as part of a shared rhythm of life they can pinpoint, between them, the most challenging areas and support and pray for one another as they identify the personal and corporate disciplines that will strengthen them to make consistent godly choices.

Character formation is the object of disciple making. It is achieved through habit, through godly repetition. It involves spiritual disciplines, but also daily obedience to the way of Christ. This commitment to a rhythm of life is helpful but it needs to be light touch, not legalistic, and should be instinctive rather than dutiful. My interest in new monasticism is, in part, because I am convinced that this sort of character formation has a much greater chance of success in community.

New monasticism is vital for the mission of the church also. Some of the newer missionary orders around today, like The Order of Mission (TOM), have drawn on monastic vows similar to the Rule of Benedict and adopted them into principles of life – hence Poverty becomes Simplicity, Obedience translates as Accountability to one another and so on. Some of our partners in the Fresh Expressions movement, CMS and Church Army, are mission agencies which are becoming Acknowledged Communities within the Church of England for the sake of their missionary calling. Another partner, 24/7 Prayer is a missionary prayer movement with a new monastic character. We shouldn't be surprised at the relevance of this approach and its effectiveness. In the era of the Celtic Church and from the time of Benedict, Europe was evangelised by monks.

I saw the results of this during an earlier period of my ministry as vicar of St Michael le Belfrey in York. York Minster, which was in my parish, was originally a minster, a community of monks who planted and later sustained churches around the area. The ancient--future nature of new monasticism means that there is much to learn from the monastic missionaries of previous eras. The sheer scale of the mission field in Britain at the moment is immense. In England, Tearfund's 2007 statistics on Churchgoing in the UK show that just over one third of adults aged 16 upwards have never had any significant link with church at all. If we include those of 15 and under we're probably heading towards half of the population. It cries out for every local church to think about a 'mixed economy' approach (a partnership of our existing patterns of church and fresh expressions); planning something different to reach those they are not reaching.

Some of us feel that the Holy Spirit may be raising up some missionary orders again to reach where the churches do not reach. These orders are not to be freelance mavericks but instead operate in a community, investing in their growth and displaying accountability to the local bishop and denominational leaders. They should act as a pool and a resource to put into those leaders' hands for the re-evangelisation of our country. There are orders which have come into existence in response to a call to mission, like TOM; and there are fresh expressions of church which sustain their life and mission by drawing on monastic sources, such as Moot in the City of London led by Ian Mobsby and Safespace in Telford led by Mark Berry. There is undoubtedly something bubbling up from the Holy Spirit and the heart of what fresh expressions is all about is seeing what God is doing locally and joining in.

Three different things could be seen to be happening in the monastic movement in England:

Some Orders with a great history are clearly in their final years. These had become small communities as their members grew older.

Other communities in better health are sometimes

overwhelmed by people who want to come on retreats or find spiritual direction. There are very substantial demands within the Church to look at these communities for spiritual guidance. All sorts of groups are seeking to develop some rule of life. This is being considered at the highest levels within the Church of England and, as I have said, involves agencies working with Fresh Expressions. These include longstanding mission agency CMS which has already made the transition to Acknowledged Community status; Church Army is on the same road; Anglican Church Planting Initiatives (ACPI) is led by Bob and Mary Hopkins, guardians of The Order of Mission; and the 24--7 prayer movement. In Lincolnshire the chairman of the local council of churches, Pete Atkins, is now developing an ecumenical order. This all shows that the connection between discipleship, mission and a community rule is increasingly understood and valued.

New monasticism is not automatically connected to a missional motive, but to the extent that it enables Christians to be authentic disciples in a changing culture, and sustain missionary movements, it can only enhance the mission of God through the Church.

Further Reading:

- Andy Freeman & Pete Greig, Punk Monk: New Monasticism and the Ancient Art of Breathing, Regal Books, 2007

- Graham Cray & Ian Mobsby (eds), Ancient Faith, Future Mission: new monasticism as fresh expression of church, Canterbury Press Norwich, 2010

- Ian Adams, Cave Refectory Road: Monastic Rhythms for contemporary living, Canterbury Press Norwich, 2010

Appendix 5

Deed of Union: Doctrine of the Methodist Church

The extract below is taken from CPD Volume 2 p. 213 which should be referred to for the full text.

Doctrine. The doctrinal standards of the Methodist Church are as follows:

Purposes. The purposes of the Methodist Church are and have been since the date of union those set out in Section 4 of the 1976 Act.

Doctrine. The doctrinal standards of the Methodist Church are as follows:

The Methodist Church claims and cherishes its place in the Holy Catholic Church, which is the Body of Christ. It rejoices in the inheritance of the apostolic faith and loyally accepts the fundamental principles of the historic creeds and of the Protestant Reformation. It ever remembers that in the providence of God Methodism was raised up to spread scriptural holiness through the land by the proclamation of the evangelical faith and declares its unfaltering resolve to be true to its divinely appointed mission.

The doctrines of the evangelical faith which Methodism has held from the beginning and still holds are based upon the divine revelation recorded in the Holy Scriptures. The Methodist Church acknowledges this revelation as the supreme rule of faith and practice. These evangelical doctrines to which the preachers of the Methodist Church are pledged are contained in Wesley's Notes on the New Testament and the first four volumes of his sermons.

The Notes on the New Testament and the 44 Sermons are not intended to impose a system of formal or speculative theology on Methodist preachers, but to set up standards of preaching and belief which should secure loyalty to the fundamental truths of the gospel of redemption and ensure the continued witness of the Church to the realities of the Christian experience of salvation.

Christ's ministers in the church are stewards in the household of God and shepherds of his flock. Some are called and ordained to this occupation as presbyters or deacons. Presbyters have a principal and directing part in these great duties but they hold no priesthood differing in kind from that which is common to all the Lord's people and they have no exclusive title to the preaching of the gospel or the care of souls. These ministries are shared with them by others to whom also the Spirit divides his gifts severally as he wills.

It is the universal conviction of the Methodist people that the office of the Christian ministry depends upon the call of God who bestows the gifts of the Spirit the grace and the fruit which indicate those whom He has chosen.

Those whom the Methodist Church recognises as called of God and therefore receives into its ministry as presbyters or deacons shall be ordained by the imposition of hands as expressive of the Church's recognition of the minister's personal call.

The Methodist Church holds the doctrine of the priesthood of all believers and consequently believes that no priesthood exists which belongs exclusively to a particular order or class of persons but in the exercise of its corporate life and worship special qualifications for the discharge of special duties are required and thus the principle of representative selection is

recognised.
All Methodist preachers are examined tested and approved before they are authorised to minister in holy things.

The Constitutional Practice and Discipline of the Methodist Church 2016